Amelia

# The Way

*Living In Love*

# THE WAY
## Living In Love

*Elena S. Whiteside*

American Christian Press
The Way International
New Knoxville, Ohio 45871

# ACKNOWLEDGEMENTS

I want to express my heartfelt thanks to Karen Martin and Donna Randall, two able and loving editors, as well as all the forces of the Print Department which were mobilized to put this volume into final form.

I also want to thank Meg Watson for the art work and Howard Yeremian for his choice photos.

And from the bottom of my heart I want to thank all those beautiful believers here, who gave of their time, their energy, their believing and of themselves to bring this book to life.

Elena S. Whiteside

Standard Book Number ISBN 0-910068-06-2
Library of Congress Catalog Card Number 72-89132
American Christian Press
ⓒ The Way International 1972
New Knoxville, Ohio 45871
Fifth Printing 1977
Printed in the United States of America

*To those who have followed*

*The Way, Jesus Christ,*

*and especially*

*To a very dedicated follower,*

*Dr. Victor Paul Wierwille*

# *Introduction*

I want to take you to a place where God is alive because people take God literally. This place will look strange to you, as strange as it did to me when I first got here, and as it sometimes still does when I recapture for a few seconds the amazement in the face of a person here for his very first time, that fleeting expression of: "What's happening here?" He hesitates, curious, pleased and utterly astounded. It's a place difficult to describe in words, and yet, you will not regret the time you spend in these pages.

I invite you to join me for a day at The Way International Headquarters in west-central Ohio, a day on the farm where the primary crop is not corn or soy beans or cattle, but the Word of God which is sown here, nourished, watered and grown in the hearts of believing people. Some people who have been here call this place "out of this world" or "a little piece of heaven on earth." Many who have been here very quickly refer to it as "home."

What is happening here is spiritual and not obvious at first glance. To the uninitiated visitor, the people here seem an ecclectic collection: old, young, middle aged, long haired, short haired, New York swagger, California cool, Mid-western homey, middle-class educated, teenage drop-out uneducated, left wing, right wing, black, white, office dress, worn-out work clothes. They come from all sections of the country, speak English with all lilts of North, South, East, West and combinations thereof. You name the classifications, and there will be someone here from that background.

What draws this diverse group together? The one great bond is oneness of spirit — their likeminded profound love of God, and belief (action) in His Word, the Bible — which completely overshadows all the minor differences.

I could go on trying to explain this to you, or I could bring to life the accuracy of the Word of God which I have been shown here, so that you could know for yourself why or how to believe God. But neither of these is my task in these pages. I want to show you God working in the lives of people. I want you to see how it looks when people actually take God and His Word at face value. I want to show you what happens in a day at The Way International, and let you see through my eyes the lives of people when God is the center of their lives.

The day I will write about is a typical day on The Way farm — a day in early spring, mid-March sometime. I could have chosen any other day, but I have chosen this one. Days are different, vary in activity, but each one is equally active. Each day here seems incredibly long in retrospect. By evening, looking back to that early morning, it seems that a year or months have gone by.

In this spiritual walk, time evaporates. Each day is a dynamic stride in growth and learning. Each day overflows with things that come to pass, with results and rejoicing, rather than unfinished business. For that is also one of God's promises: If a person does things putting God first, he gets results. The day I describe may sound impossible to you, or like a special day, gorged with activity, and yet, everyday is like this one. It is the truth. And if you can't believe it, come and see for yourself. You are more than welcome to visit here.

In this book, you will meet many people. On this particular day in March, there are forty people living here together. I'd like you to meet every one of them, to look into their peaceful eyes, basque in their heart-felt smiles and hear from their own lips the stories of how they came to this place, of the miracles that revolutionized each one of their lives. But time and space do not permit me to put each person's own story in this book. And yet, I cannot avoid introducing a cross-section of these people to you. To bring you close to only a few of these people does not mean that only those dozen are the most important ones here. Rather they are representative and they were just the ones who fell in with me on this day. By the time you read this book, many of these people will have gone out into the field, taken on heavier responsibilities or moved to different positions; however, the love and believing here does not change.

There is not space in this book for each one of the forty to bloom; but there is one person who will be given special coverage. That person is the man who for thirty years researched the Word of God and then was able with enthusiasm and conviction to share it with the people here and many others around the country and the rest of the world. It is this man's stand over the years, his believing in the Word of God, that started The Way ministry. God gives the increase, but someone has to believe His Word and act on it for God to come through with results. The man who initially believed was Dr. Victor Paul Wierwille.

Dr. Wierwille is no one superhuman or inherently special. He is only human like the rest of us. The hero of the people in this place is God, not Dr. Wierwille, but their exposure to God came through the teaching and example of Dr. Wierwille. It is not Dr. Wierwille's native brilliance or ability that makes him stand out among other men. History is full of great brains and great talents. It is rather his willingness to truly put God above all else which makes him able to receive and put into practice the Word of God. It is this love of God that he manifests daily in the smallest instances that you will encounter here.

Before I take you to this place for a day, let me clarify one more point. The only perfection is God, His Word, and His Son Jesus Christ. People on this earth are just not perfect, and neither is this ministry perfect. I make no such claims for this ministry or the people in it. However, there is no where else I have seen, heard or read about in this world, where people are getting together according to the accuracy of God's Word, living, working, rejoicing, helping, teaching, healing broken hearts, bodies and minds, and growing together in love. This is the work of Jesus Christ. He is God's Way. And this book is a day with the part of the Body of Christ living at The Way Headquarters. A similar day could be spent anywhere else with any group of believers who are walking on the Word of God.

God is the hero of this book. And God is the hero of the people that live in these pages. But God is Spirit. Spirit cannot be discerned through the five senses. It cannot be seen or heard, touched, tasted or smelled. (Spirit is spirit and the senses realm is the senses realm.) I cannot show you spirit, point it out, isolate it or frame it. But the hero of this story is still God. Does that sound impossible?

I cannot show you God face to face, but I can show you God working and living in people. I can show you people who believe God and act on that believing. I can show you people acting on the Word of God and living according to His Word. People who believe produce acts, and I can show you acts.

Perhaps you want to see more coming to pass in your life, more results. God is willing and able to walk with you too. But you have to decide yourself that you want to walk with God. And if you do, God and you are the heavies in any situation. If you are interested, searching, curious, discouraged, or simply enjoy seeing something different, something out of this world, then share this day with me and see some people who walk God's way.

*Elena S. Whiteside*

# Morning

*Morning*

"*A* sower went out to sow his seed: and as he sowed, some fell by the wayside; and it was trodden down, and the fowls of the air devoured it.

And some fell upon a rock; and as soon as it sprung up, it withered away, because it lacked moisture.

And some fell among thorns; and the thorns sprang up with it and choked it.

And other fell on good ground, and bare fruit an hundredfold. And when he [Jesus] had said these things, he cried, He that hath ears to hear, let him hear.

And his disciples asked him saying, What might this parable be?

And he said, Unto you it is given to know the mysteries of the kingdom of God; but to others in parables; that seeing they might not see, and hearing they might not understand.

Now the parable is this: **The seed is the word of God.** Those by the wayside are they that hear; then cometh the devil and taketh away the word out of their hearts, lest they should believe and be saved.

They on the rock are they, which when they hear receive the word with joy; and these have no root, which for a while believe, and in time of temptation fall away. And that which fell among thorns are they, which when they have heard, go forth, and are choked with cares and riches and pleasures of this life and bring no fruit to perfection.

But that on the good ground are they which in an honest and good heart, having heard the word, keep it and bring forth fruit with patience."

Luke 8:5-15

The Way is a place where the Word of God fell upon good ground, where people hear the Word, keep it and bring forth fruit with patience. The Way Biblical Research Center is a 147-acre farm in the heartland of America. In the fertile, brown soil of Ohio, the seed of the Word of God fell upon good ground.

It is early morning. From my window in Trailer 5, I can see the vast expanse of flat land, stripped of last summer's crops, stretching into the sky. On the horizon thin, wispy forests of trees, admit the early morning sky through their branches.

Across the fields of hacked down corn stalks in one direction I can see another farm just like this one in the naked brown fields. Several buildings cluster about a silver silo now catching the first rays of early morning sun. Its lustrous yellow domed roof glitters like some Byzantine cathedral in the distance. The main house and barn, easily distinguishable by their size, are surrounded by a handful of smaller buildings. The farm is the basic unit in these agricultural parts.

Brown and yellow tinges of winter still linger in the land and small islands of snow from yesterday's sudden blizzard still lie in the shade of the larger fir trees. It is before six o'clock. The wind moans around the north corner of the trailer mournfully.

The Way farm is basically like the one I can see from my window. The main barn still bears on its roof the faded but legible letters clearly reading: "A. E. Wierwille 1891." The main house, a two story structure of white wood, stands a little apart, surrounded by grassy lawns. Several smaller build-ings, a garage workshop, another old barn, now used as a garage and snackshop, the loft, housing students in the sum-mer, and tool sheds make up the original farm.

Besides these, in neat rows, over a dozen mobile homes house the people that live here today. One is the men's trailer, another the women's trailer, each housing about 20 in close but comfortable quarters. Beyond that, married couples and families live in the other mobile homes. Another trailer contains the Main Office, and still another the Collating Department.

There are several unheated cottages used for storage in the winter and for campers in the summer. By the road there is a good-sized house presently occupied by the general manager of The Way, Howard Allen, his wife and five children.

Does it sound like a hodge podge of structures? The amaz-ing thing is that the effect is not cluttered, busy or over-crowded. And I have to add to these the large but low-roofed Biblical Research Center, the heart of daily life here with teaching in the auditorium upstairs, while the cooking and eating take place in the basement downstairs.

The latest addition to the farm is the new executive office building, still under construction. But we'll get a closer look at all these places later.

The overall effect is neatness and order and an extremely efficient use of space without overcrowding. It is still a work-ing farm, with sheep and horses, corn fields on either side, a pond with geese, ducks and swans, a dog kennel, containing several yapping hunting dogs, tractors in the shed and gardens in the back.

It is a midwestern working farm, and yet, how much more besides. As I said before, the main crop here is not corn or soy beans, but the sowing of the Word of God, building it into the lives of men and women, who in turn reap and distribute a vast spiritual harvest.

It is early morning, around six. The birds twitter today even in the cold. From my room I hear the rooster crowing with gusto in the barn. The doors open and slam shut on trailers 6 and 7, followed by the muffled exchange of voices and a tripping of hurried footsteps over the little wooden bridge that straddles a low area on the way to the Biblical Research Center. The day has begun.

It is bitter cold this morning again, for in March the weather is changeable here. A warm spell enveloped us a few days ago followed by yesterday's sudden blizzard. On my way to the Biblical Research Center, referred to as the Bible Center by the students, I shove my hands deep into my coat pockets to save them from tingling in the chill of early morning air. To the southeast beside the main house, heavy yellow and pink clouds mellow the sky in that rich diffuse light of the Midwest. An atmosphere of peace and purpose pervades the grounds.

My footsteps ring hollowly on the red brick path. A few more people pass me on their way to the Bible Center to begin each day as they end it, in fellowship and in prayer.

The door opens into a warm alcove. Downstairs in the student lounge the eight W.O.W. ambassadors are gathering for their early morning meeting.

Let me clarify something before I go on. The Bible says anyone who believes is an ambassador for Christ, so any believer is an ambassador. However, these eight W.O.W. ambassadors and over a hundred others all over the country and abroad are people who have made a one-year commitment to stand and hold forth the Word of God. (W.O.W. stands for "Word Over the World.") W.O.W. ambassadors are expected to support themselves by part-time jobs and then witness eight hours a day. Their responsibilities include establishing fellowships and teaching biblical research classes.

The eight here this morning were given a Headquarters assignment where they do necessary work as well as study, learn and grow spiritually strong. Their program is designed to build discipline, knowledge of God's Word and commitment.

There's Meg, a tall brunette with snappy sassoon hair cut, who comes from New York where she had been a successful commercial artist. Now 23, she preferred to leave worldly success behind for the satisfaction of doing her craft toward spreading The Word visually. She works eight hours a day in all visual media: posters, signs, coloring books, cartoons, book covers, record jackets. Her art work is everywhere on the walls of the Biblical Research Center and the offices.

Beside her is Becky from Wichita, another brunette, 20 years old, with a dimpled smile, who was brought up as a

Mennonite before she found The Way. She works cleaning 8 hours a day, keeping the Biblical Research Center, offices and meeting rooms meticulously clean, as they always are.

Dave, the tall blonde Californian, is in charge of the garage workshop, repairing and maintaining cars and machinery. Sammy from Kansas is the coordinator of the eight ambassadors here on the farm. He, Tom and Sky all work as carpenters or as laborers doing whatever needs to be done.

Then there's Steve who specializes in electrical work and air-conditioning. Beside him this morning sits Doug, the only one of the guys with short hair. Doug, from North Carolina, is in charge of planning and organizing the Rock of Ages, a yearly summer rock festival. His job has a myriad of details to keep track of 15,000 kids as are expected this August for Rock of Ages '72.

"Let's get with the exercises," Sammy begins, and the eight move slowly into an empty section of the basement. Running through a series of calisthenics, they end up doing a hundred jumping jacks, increasing the speed with every jump. Smiling and winded, they settle themselves back into the student lounge furniture, each one pulling out his Bible. Doug stifles a yawn and then Meg. After all, it is very early in the morning and the ambassadors do with six hours sleep a night.

Only the sound of heavy breathing disturbs the stillness for a moment, and then from the kitchen on the other side of the Biblical Research Center basement, sounds of breakfast —

dishes jangling, spoons in pots, electric can opener whirring — creep into us seated in a circle in the alcove.

Sammy begins (as coordinator of the eight ambassadors on the farm, he is expected to take things in hand), "Why don't you lead the meeting this morning, Sky."

Sky shakes his dark, wavy midway-to-shoulder-length hair back from his face. In spite of his mustache, his face is youthful. He is only slightly surprised, but ready as any one of the people in that room would have been, ready at a second's notice to lead a meeting or share something from God's Word with enthusiasm and knowledge.

Sky straightens his back, takes a deep breath, looking from one to another in the circle with him. "Let's start with prayer. Anyone of you who wants just lift what's on your heart, and we'll pray with you. We'll have a season of prayer and then manifestations, and then I'll share something from the Word with you." He lays out the order and direction of the meeting. There are any number of ways to do it, but that is where the leader takes responsibility. He lays it out.

These prayer sessions, even though they occur a number of times during the day among various groups of people, are always different, always spontaneous, always imbued with the spiritual power that comes from a group of people totally likeminded about whatever is being prayed for in those few minutes. Prayer is believing God and knowing He will bring things to pass.

Doug begins by lifting the Rock of Ages, that it will not be hindered in any way, that all the plans will work smoothly and everyone who goes will be uplifted, blessed and strengthened. He lifts all the transportation and facilities, the joy and order of the crowd and the greatness of the music.

Sky lifts the other ambassadors all over the country, that they are strengthened and comforted wherever they are, whatever they are doing. Meg lifts Dr. Wierwille, his family, and Dave, the ministry and men and women of God here and all over the country, that they walk today in power, love and wisdom.

There is a pause and then Sky speaks: "Will someone please bring a message from God." Everyones eyes are tightly shut and there is an air of heavy expectancy.

"My beloved children, walk forth in this day boldly on my Word knowing that I will strengthen every step. I shall guide you, for my love for you is very great, even beyond your understanding, and I shall never leave you nor forsake you."

"Someone else, please."

"Verily, verily, I say unto you, hold forth my Word and be fearless, for I shall let no harm come to you. You shine as lights in a crooked and perverse nation; just shine and the darkness about you shall be dispelled."

The tenor of the meeting changes from quiet calm to an inner excitement as the messages continue. The knowledge that God is speaking directly to this group here today, never fails to build everyone to a great spiritual crescendo, from which they emerge literally bubbling with enthusiasm and joy.

Sammy says a prayer of thanks and praise to God. Then grinning widely, Sky opens his Bible. The group is quiet, yet smiling and animated, happy to be alive.

"I want to read with you from I Thessalonians this morning," Sky begins. His voice has a note of authority, boldness yet without pride but with heartfelt humility. In his patched and faded blue jeans, and gray work shirt, dressed for a day of hard work, he reads with great respect to us from the Word of God. He reads as though he knows in the depths of his soul that clothes and outward appearance are not what count, but God looks on the heart.

Everyone else follows his reading with unblinking interest. He reads from chapter 4 of I Thessalonians and, coming to the section on Christ's return, breaks out into a broad smile: " 'For the Lord himself shall descend from heaven with a shout ....' Boy, that's going to be the greatest day of our lives. Isn't it fantastic? He's going to descend from heaven with a shout. We'll know it." And everyone nods at one another in eye-sparkling enthusiasm, for they all believe it.

Sky finishes reading the section, comments on a few phrases to bring them to our attention, and then closes his eyes simultaneously. "Let's have a closing prayer," and then he thanks God for "this beautiful day, for our perfect health and sound minds, and that everyone is going to have a fantastic day, getting a lot accomplished for the Lord, through Jesus Christ."

That's it. The meeting is over. There's a wave of stretching, eye rubbing, deep breathing around the room, and the ambassadors have a few moments of rest before breakfast.

They meet every morning as I have said, but that is not the only early meeting. Upstairs in the main hall of the Biblical Research Center, twenty-five Way Corps members meet together at the same early hour.

Unlike the ambassadors, who have a one-year commitment to stand and hold forth the Word wherever they are, who are prepared on a day or even on a one-hour notice to move from one city to another as they are needed, the Way Corps members have made a two-year commitment to work with The Way ministry. For these two years they live here on the farm, building in themselves discipline and knowledge of the Word of God. They are learning to be leaders and after their two years here will be able to lead in the work of this ministry in all parts of the country. Some go out for periods of a few weeks to run classes, and all of them go out to nearby groups to teach and witness.

Each member works four hours a day in the various facets of the ministry: Printing Department, mailing, collating new materials, translations, shop, carpentry, office and administration — with films, with tapes or typing. In addition, they study and research by themselves, and evenings are devoted to teaching and witnessing, as well as learning in special seminars.

This morning the Corps has gathered together as every morning. Dressed in navy blue or grey sweatsuits, hoods flopping back, hair hastily pinned up or back, they fill up most of the room. Yet there is no feeling of overcrowding, but of peace as Del Duncan asks for an opening prayer. One by one several pray, spontaneously with an air of looseness and freedom, and at the same time, intense concentration.

Eight of the group are in their second year, ready to graduate and be assigned out at the end of this summer, and seventeen are in their first year. The age range is just under twenty to almost thirty. Del, at twenty-five is the coordinator of the entire group. He and his blonde wife, Nancy, are both in the Corps, their two-year-old son Aaron in no way hindering their participation. In her seventh month of pregnancy, Nancy still takes active part in nearly all the activities.

This morning she prays also in her thin but firm voice: "And Father, thank you that we can today look at you through eyes fresh with excitement at your greatness, and not just take you for granted because nothing can separate us from the love you have for us. Your Word says so. Thank you that we can know this. Thank you for the life you have given us and for your constant and unending kindness to us. You always give us that second, third and fourth chance. How can we do less for others when we know you will continue in your love and tenderness towards us? Thank you for this great day to walk for you, through your Son and our Savior Christ Jesus."

Craig, the tall blond leader of the first-year Corps, a college graduate from Oklahoma, prays for everyone's families: "You know, God, how much they mean to us, and thank you for their lives."

Several others pray, and then Del calls for manifestations of the spirit. The boldness of the words electrifies the air. The messages generate a spiritual excitement, a sharpness of mind and wide-awake attitude. And then Del leads the group in exercises. His two years in the Navy, his years spent hustling through the drug world, and his year running on the periphery of the Hell's Angels have all contributed to his understanding of people, making him an effective leader. His manner is unassuming, loose and with much humor, winning him trust and confidence. But it is his total commitment and dedication to the Word of God that wins him the respect and enthusiastic cooperation of those about him.

Now he stands up his full six-foot height, his blond hair just long enough to bounce as he touches his toes: "One, two, three for the Lord. Four, five, six for his glory." Everyone touches his toes, stretches out, loosens up, repeated again and again, and Del throws in a bit of his early morning humor: "Did you hear about the lady who bought a Playtex living bra?" Pause, as everyone waits panting for the punch line. "Well, it bit her." He raises his voice above the guffaws. "OK, let's break up into our two groups now. Guys over here with me, and girls on the other side with Tim. Let's go."

Almost instantly the two groups have formed, and Tim, who had spent some time studying dance before joining the Corps, has launched into a series of modern dance loosening-up exercises. He flows right from one into another, hardly pausing between them, and throwing in 30 push-ups or 20 sit-ups between dance movements.

Del leads the men through an even more strenuous series of calisthenics, beginning with 77 sit-ups, push-ups, bicycling, more sit-ups, more push-ups, backward push-ups, back to sit-ups, not stopping to catch his breath or to wipe the sweat off his face. The faces turn cherry red and bright pink with effort, and a few groans and heaves escape from straining jaws, but everyone has an abundance of determination.

"OK, that's it," Del calls above the sounds of effort exerted, "Let's have a closing word of prayer, somebody."

The clock on the wall shows seven even. Silence fills the room, and Bo's voice rises breaking the stillness: "Thank you, Father, for the chance to work and strengthen our bodies for you. Thank you for perfect health today and that we may stay alert and on top of every situation this entire day through Christ Jesus in us. Amen."

He ends on an upbeat. Without hesitation, the twenty-five break into conversation, turning, laughing, gesturing to each other. "God bless you," "Good morning," "Hi, don't you look wonderful today," "Bless you," "See you at breakfast." Everyone greets each other with unforced brightness, on their way to change or shower before breakfast at 7:15. The room is quickly emptied.

From the kitchen directly below, hot and tasty smells filter through the building. Today Debbie alone has cooked breakfast for the 40 people. She stands over a giant pot of hot yellow mush. The tables are neatly set already by the dish crew from the night before. The china is simple, white with a thin gold rim, yet in good taste.

Each table is crowned with a huge bowl of bright oranges, and today there are smaller bowls of raïsins and flax seeds served with the corn mush. Four tables are set up, each one seating ten people. Green and yellow insulated pitchers of hot coffee, and cold milk and ice water are always on the tables, but the menus change. There is always something fresh to eat (fruit) and something hearty (oatmeal, homemade familia, French toast or pancakes). All the meals are basically simple, hearty and well-thought-out.

The atmosphere at meals is cheerful, full of warmth. Mealtimes are a time to fellowship together, steeped in the sharing of enjoyment and relaxation. Although cooked for a large group, meals are always prompt, always distinctly home-cooked and not institutional in flavor, and always served steaming hot. Two cooks handle the food preparation every day. Debbie was in today at 6 o'clock, another cook, Louise or Eileen, will join her at eight to prepare the other meals.

Well, you may be saying to yourself at this point as we are about to sit down to breakfast at 7:15, "So what?" Surely there are other groups of people living harmoniously and working together; surely there are other places where the food is good, and served punctually; surely there are other people who get up early and pray together, or do exercises early in the morning.

I must agree. There surely are. And yet this place and these people here and now are unlike any group I have come in contact with either in college, in graduate school, in hospitals, in offices on projects where I have worked, in clubs I have been associated with, or in families, my own or others.

What is so outstandingly different? Writing has its limitations. I cannot quote or describe every single detail or every conversation, even in one day, no matter how alert and comprehensive my observations. But one great difference between this group and others in the world is the total lack of negatives.

Have you ever sat down and taken stock of the conversations about you, or your own for that matter? What is it? Mostly negative. It's "I can't do this," or "Isn't this terrible," or "I'm afraid I can't," or "Why on earth did this or that happen?" or "Did you read about this or that in the news?" — and the news itself is just about all negative.

And that is one thing almost totally lacking here that you will find in other groups of people together — the negatives. Not only the overt negatives are absent, but also the covert ones, the hidden resistance you see and feel in the gritting of teeth behind the reluctant "All right, I'll do it if I have to," or the downcast face behind the "Why does it always have to be me?" or the annoyed tone in the "I'll try to do it later, or tomorrow."

You may think that I have left out the complaining, the gossip, the everyday annoyances, the interpersonal sarcasm. This day here may seem exaggerated to you or superficial. Well, I have left them out, because they are not here to record. And if this seems hard for you to believe, I can only reiterate my invitation: Come and see for yourself.

Active believing in God produces a totally positive atmosphere. When needs come up whether they be personal ones, a need for comfort, or for encouragement, or material ones, such as a need for cleaning a room or fixing a car or repairing a leaky roof or washing a wall or planting the fields in season or for the construction of a new dormitory, the needs are immediately met here. Things are handled in a positive way for God has promised us results. The people here, believing God together for the results, get results.

Furthermore, God is a God of order. Life here reflects that order. Without the negatives, people here are able to put all their energy into doing what has to be done in an orderly fashion. A sense of order pervades the grounds and all the activities. There is order, yet without coercion, repression, suppression or oppression from outside sources.

The order is based on awareness and developing self-discipline. Each person here is committed to this ministry and likeminded on its basis — the Word of God. The order here is obvious but looks effortless to anyone who comes on the grounds. A great deal of planning and effort goes into it, but the energy goes into the doing of it rather than talking about it — into getting it done, rather than dragging one's feet about it.

I believe you will notice these qualities emerge throughout this day: the positive atmosphere, the order and the general likemindedness. These qualities are hard to find in the out-side world, and they are what make possible the tremendous volume of work that is accomplished here daily.

But let us return to breakfast. Debbie, in her faded-blue jeans set off by a brightly embroidered blouse, her light brown hair pinned up on her head in a bun, has set the last bowl of steaming corn mush on the table. People stand around talking quietly. Someone has just dozed off on the couch. (I can't quite see who it is.) Nancy Bowen, the slender dark-haired hostess with a serious face as she oversees the smooth running of the entire dining room, is raising her hand to indicate silence. Conversation drops off momentarily.

"Let's all find seats now," she directs us. There is a moment of relocation, shuffling, as each person finds a chair. "Del, would you have the blessing, please?"

"Well, Father, we surely thank you for blessing this food to the strength of our bodies, and thank you for blessing the hands that prepared it, and those who paid for it. Thank you for a great day today through Christ Jesus. Amen." Everyone joins in the "Amen" heartily, and with a scraping of chairs, the men seat the women and then sit down themselves.

Yes, there is an insistence on manners here, on Christian etiquette. It's nice to do it right, and it's nice to know how to behave with propriety or with dignity in any situation. This teaching of manners annoyed me when I first arrived here last summer, until one young woman told me how thankful she was to learn. "You see, I never learned at home," she explained. "We just all fed ourselves from the refrigerator when we got hungry. That's how my mother ran her home. But consequently, when I grew up and got away from home, I had a terrible fear of eating out or even eating with any other person. You can imagine what a bondage that was. My friends would all go out after a game, or after the movie or something, and I just didn't have the courage to go with them because I was so embarassed to have anyone see my stupidities at the table. Until I got here. I'm so grateful someone took the time, the patience and insistence to teach me how to eat right. It liberated me from fear and shame. Now I can go out, eat with anyone, knowing I'm not going to make a terrible fool of myself. It's so great to be free of that bondage of ignorance."

She gave me a hearty smile, an unfettered toss of her head, and we talked about something else. I don't even recall her name as it was my first day or two here, but I vividly remember her statement and her appreciation for instruction in manners. That conversation totally reversed my lingering annoyance with emphasis on table manners and introductions. I suddenly realized that manners and etiquette can be ways of relating in love to people. If you don't know how to show consideration, you can learn how, and then knowing how releases you to conduct yourself graciously or not as you choose. Now I see that the insistence on Christian etiquette here is meeting an important need in people, especially for those who simply never learned elsewhere.

At each table, the food is passed around clockwise, everyone helping himself. A host sits at one end, a hostess at the other directing the operation by asking someone to start the oranges around, someone else the cereal, someone else the seeds, raisins, milk, coffee, honey and raw sugar. When everyone at the table has served himself, we begin to eat.

However, this is not the only breakfast now happening on the farm. The families eat at home: Dr. Wierwille breakfasts with his wife and two youngest children, John Paul, 16, and

Sara, 14, every morning before they go to school. Howard Allen, the general manager, eats with his wife and five children. Gene Randall, the farm manager, breakfasts with his wife, Donna, who is on the research staff and his high school-age son, the other two daughters being in college. Ermal Owens, Vice-President of The Way and his wife, Dorothy, director of admissions, live and take meals in their own mobile home. All these families reside here on the grounds also, leading close family lives, and yet participating in the greater family that lives and works here. The Word says God is our Father and we are His children. All those who believe are of the **household** of God. And that is indeed what it is like here, a great big family.

But let's hurry back to our plates filled with hot mush, smothered with sesame seeds, raisins, milk and honey. Del is the host at our table today. Little Aaron sits in a high chair, covered with a plastic bib, and Nancy sits on his other side. Inconspicuous, Aaron is surrounded by love from both his parents and all the other believers here.

Across from me Tim is talking to two guests who arrived late last night. Paul and Angie were on their way to go skiing in Colorado, stopped by to see Tim, a classmate of Paul's in high school, and have decided to stay here to learn more. And that is not uncommon. People drop by to see, and then stay on, so taken are they by what is manifested and available here.

"You came just at the right time," Tim is saying with unabashed enthusiasm. "There is a class starting here this weekend if you really want to know more. To know God's will you have to know His Word, and that is what that class will open up for you. When God made man, he didn't just make him and then leave him to blunder about on his own. God made a handbook to go along with man, and that handbook is the Bible. It contains all that we have to know to lead a more abundant life. Not just scraping by, coming up now and then for air, but the best possible life for us. That's what God put in His Word — what is available to us right now. If you don't know what's available, you just can't use it."

Paul and Angie listen attentively as Tim talks.

"What is this class you're talking about? Is that the one you told me about a while ago, the one you were taking?" Paul asks very seriously.

"It's called 'Power for Abundant Living,'" Tim continues. "It's the class that changed my life. It's a foundational class, giving you the keys to understanding God's Word. Thirty-three hours of straight teaching, but they do it over three weeks here, so that you go four evenings a week, for three hours each time. It's fantastic because when you've had it, you'll be able to understand what God wants us to know. I was looking for God everywhere and missing Him everywhere, 'til I took that class. Nowhere else can you get this knowledge of how to read and understand God's Word. And the thing you just can't deny about it is that it works. Apply the principles and you get the results in your life."

Tim sits back, breaking into a broad grin and adds: "But that's enough; you've heard enough. I won't say anymore. How's old ... from high school? Have you heard from him recently?" Tim inquires about their mutual friend with the same enthusiasm and intense interest he had for describing the class. In fact, whatever he does, whether leading the girls in early morning exercises, or having breakfast, or talking about old friends, he is dynamically and joyfully involved.

Paul considers his words and answers carefully. He has short dark hair, glasses, smooth skin and a collegiate air. Beside him Angie, her black eyes glistening, listens seriously. Part Cuban and part Spanish, her dark olive skin gives her a foreign flavor, even though she grew up and lived most of her life in New York.

But the conversation does not veer far off for Paul has questions on his mind, and brings them up to Tim. "What makes this place any different from some other denomination? What's so different about how this place is run or organized?" he ventures.

"You see, denominations are man-made," Tim begins. "Here we learn what God says and we do things according to His Word. This is the closest thing you'll find to the first century Church anywhere in the world. The Church in the Bible is the body of people who believe. It's not a building or a denomination, but the people who believe and act on the Word of God. In the first century these people met in private houses, and it was there in those small fellowships of believers that the needs of people were really met on a one-to-one basis. The Church was highly personal. They broke bread together, they prayed together, they tithed their money and everything they didn't need, and they praised God from house to house. You can read all about it in the book of

Acts. Each fellowship had an elder, a leader, someone in
charge. Now these elders in an area would get together and
believe God to choose one of them to be spiritually responsible." Tim pauses momentarily to find the exact words.

"That's how we are organized. You see, we are not a
denomination. There's no membership because the life and
growth of this ministry is in the twigs. That's what we call
these small fellowships in private homes: twig fellowships.
Any one who wants to learn or hear or share the Word of
God can come to a twig meeting. We gather around the Word
of God. Wherever two or three are gathered together, Jesus
Christ said He would be in their midst."

"But that's a funny name, 'twig'," Angie interposes suddenly. "What does that mean?"

"I guess it does sound funny," Tim flashes a smile. "We're
so used to it around here. You see, a twig comes from a tree,
and that was the Doctor's vision for this ministry years ago,
that it is like a tree, and the life of a tree is in its twigs. The
twig is that little fellowship of believers that I was telling you
about, that meets in people's private homes once or twice or
three times a week. Two or three get together and they bring
in people who are interested in hearing the Word, and that's
how the twig grows. Each new person is like a new leaf. When
you see a tree, what do you see first? You don't say, 'Oh,
what a beautiful trunk,' or 'What a great twig.' You see the
leaves. That's what you see in this ministry, too — the people.
And you know, the twig grows when it is tender. It is the
tenderness, the love that the new people see in us that draws
them. And it is the tenderness that makes the twig spring

forth with new leaves. A hardened twig doesn't continue growing. When a twig gets too big, then it splits up into two others, and when they grow, they split. That's how the ministry grows too.

"Now take an area. Like Rye, New York where I come from. You've been to Rye," Tim says, leaning slightly closer to Paul. "There are dozens of twig meetings there every week in different homes; and not just in Rye, but in Larchmont and in New Rochelle, and Peekskill and Croton. That's only a few of the places. There are a lot more.

"When there are at least three twigs in one area, they form a branch which is coordinated by a leader. And several branches together form a limb. The limb leader is spiritually responsible for a whole area. The Way East limb is in Rye. They organize special classes, they get the class materials, hold seminars, make available the Sunday night meeting which is just like here, every Sunday night. There's a limb in California called The Way West, one in Kansas, Indiana, North Carolina and lots of states, and the limbs are attached to the trunk. The trunk is the central coordinating point for the whole United States. Other trunks would be in other countries. We have fellowships in Sweden, in England and Australia now.

"The roots of the tree are right here in the International Headquarters. It is here that the research is done, that the materials are made available. From here the teachings go out on tapes. This root feeds the whole tree with the newest research on the Word of God.

"But there is no membership. It's all your free will. There's no coercion. People come together because they love the Word and they love to come together and share and learn and build up one another and rejoice in what God has done for us. They come because they see life in the twig and in the tree — life, love and the power of God." Tim pauses, immensely exhilarated.

"Doctor did a fantastic teaching on the Way Tree just last week at the Sunday night meeting. That's when everyone from miles around comes here to learn. There are usually several hundred here for that. Tapes are made of the teaching and sent out the next day to all the limb leaders, branch leaders and to others, like the ambassadors all over the country. You'll be here next Sunday, and you'll see. It's great. Everyone gets really high on the Word together.

"You see, the Word says that we, the believers in His Word, are the Body of Christ. We are the Body of Christ, and Christ Himself is the head. The Body of Christ is made up of lots and lots of people, not just here, but wherever someone believes the Word of God. And when everyone gets together on a Sunday night, you can just feel it and see it, the Body beats with one heart, and breathes the same breath. When there are so many together like that and everyone knows that they are one spirit, it's just beautiful.

"You'll see for yourself next Sunday. Sunday meetings are great, here or at Rye or California, Kansas, Indiana, wherever they are. But still, the life and growth of the ministry are in the twigs. It's where the everyday needs are met. We comfort one another, exhort, encourage, reprove, correct, answer questions from the Word. You see, we do it. It's the Word of God in us that heals, that gives knowledge and wisdom, strength and hope. Where else in the world do you find all those things rolled up in one book?

"Oh, I could go on and on about the Word. You can see that. I get so excited when it comes to the Word of God. Boy, and the greatest thing about it is that it works every time. But what the Doctor teaches in that class in 33 hours I couldn't teach you in 33 hours. He's been doing research and teaching for 30 years now and he's a terrific teacher. That class will give you the foundation, the keys to understanding God's Word. It'll really blow your mind. The depth of that class is just tremendous."

Paul smiles a little reservedly in the face of Tim's out-and-out enthusiasm. "Well, I'm ready to take it. I don't know if what you're saying will hold for me, but I sure have been searching for something. I've tried a whole lot of trips and all of them petered out after a while. I'll stay the three weeks and take the class."

"So will I. I'm ready to hear more," Angie remarks quietly. "It sounds great. I can't believe it—that it's that great, I mean — but I want to hear more."

There's a silent wave of rejoicing at our table. No one says much, but everone has been blessed. Tim regards them both with great warmth. "After breakfast let's go see Howard Allen about a place for you to stay while you're here. Howard will know. I'll go over with you." Tim takes his first mouthful of breakfast. It's already cold, but he doesn't seem to mind.

There is one other category of people here at breakfast whom I have not as yet mentioned. Besides the twenty-five Way Corps members and eight ambassadors, the rest of the people here are staff or workers. They are here to do specific work for the ministry such as typing and carpentry. Working a full day, they spend their evenings also in study, at fellowships or teaching and in general building up themselves spiritually.

Two of them are at our table this morning. Beside me is Claudettee, a twenty-year-old black woman from Kansas. You can always tell where Claudettee is sitting at meals by the laughter at the table for her quips are constant. However, she was not invited here to amuse the believers, but as a typist eight hours a day in the office — although that's not her only function here either. Gifted with a rich, mellow contralto voice, she is one of the pillars of the music ministry. Having left behind a full music scholarship at college, many singing awards and honors in Kansas, she now sings here at Sunday night meetings as well as at other functions. And she has just cut her first record of inspirational songs on the Almond Tree label.

Across from Claudettee, Susan, a fair-haired Southerner, has recently returned from eight months of working in a missionary hospital in Africa. Susan's specialty is sewing. Her workday now consists of sewing volumes of draperies for the new executive office building, besides sewing clothes for people living here.

"I just want to know if the oranges this morning are sweet," Susan is saying, contemplating the orange in front of her. "You know, some of them are and some of them aren't. How is yours, Claudettee?"

"Eat it. You'll see for yourself," Claudettee urges her. "They're fine. I'd just call them imitation lemons."

Already some people have finished. Breakfast is the only meal at which people are excused individually as they are finished. Everyone clears away his own dishes at breakfast. Several from our table have left already. But I like to linger and absorb the warmth, the fellowship, the delightful early morning greetings and compliments. It is a family, a large and wonderful, varied family, held tenderly together by the love of God.

Del is filling his plate again, and, knowing he will be here a while, I ask him about his life before he got into the Word.

"It's a long story, but I love to tell it," he responds cheerfully. His yellow hair falls neatly just under his ears and his blue eyes are clear and unwavering.

"I grew up in Oklahoma, was in and out of trouble through high school, and ended up in reform school for a couple of years. When I was sixteen, I ran away from home and lived around with aunts and uncles. But by 18, I was getting in heavy scenes with my friends. We attempted some robberies and got caught. So I was brought up before the judge, and he gave us a choice of prison for juvenile delinquents or joining the service.

"So naturally I enlisted for four years in the Navy. I enlisted for four years, but I only ended up staying a year and a half. You see, that was when the Vietnam thing was building up. I was a Medical Corpsman, and I knew I didn't want to go over there. I had a friend with me, Mike Martin, so he and I devised a plan to play crazy.

"Our other choice was to play homosexual, but we decided that was no good because it would lead to a dishonorable discharge. Then Mike had a plan — we should make like we were freaking out on acid. So that's what we did. We'd worked with psychedelics before, so we knew what they wanted to hear. It totally fooled them and the whole base was investigated by order from the Pentagon. We'd be called in to be questioned, but we had our tactics all worked out already. We'd rat on each other and accuse each other.

"One night, they had a raid on our barracks — lights, banging, rifles in the middle of the night. The whole trip. They made us all get out of bed, searched us and then searched all our private belongings. They searched everything, and the funny thing was that they found drugs on everyone, *everyone*, in that room, except on Mike and me. We were clean.

"Well, in spite of that small success, things went on and on, without moving ahead. So one day during a maneuver, I sat down and refused to go anywhere. They called the officer, and then another officer. I just refused to move, and finally they sent me to the 'psyche.' He was cool. He talked to me for a while, questioned me real cool, and then he said: 'I know you're bluffing.' Just like that. For a second, I thought it was all lost. I thought that he had really called my bluff, but then I just flashed on it: It's either now or never. If he doesn't believe me, I gotta make one last push. So then I just freaked out. Completely. I just ran all around the room throwing everything on the floor — his diplomas, the pictures, just everything — ending up crouched and cowering under his desk. The guy was pretty amazed, and that got me into the psychic ward for a while, and I finally got my discharge.

"By then Mike was on the other side of the country, but the funny thing was, he was discharged the very same day and hour I was. That was in 1966. Mike and I met in California after being discharged and both got into drugs together, shooting speed and stuff. But it was bad. I knew it was bad. I got down to 107 pounds, and I'm over six feet tall. I was physically wasted so I decided to quit. I made one last big deal and went to stay with my sister in Detroit.

"But that was no good either, so I left there and came back to California and bluffed my way into an inhalation therapy job. I knew a lot from my medical training in the Navy, and as soon as I was in, I learned fast. I got Mike into it too. I was making a lot of money, so I got a big house on the beach and invited all my friends to come there and get off drugs. But it didn't work out. I just got back on. We had nothing solid, nothing to stand on.

"That January of 1968, the house folded. I lost my job because I was spaced all the time and I had ended up supporting the house because everyone else was so spaced all the time. It's like that thing the Doctor tells on one of the tapes. It's funny, how if you put one rotten apple into a barrel of good apples, they all turn rotten; but when you put a good apple into a barrel of rotten apples, they don't all turn good.

Not that I was a good apple. I'd just seen what drugs did to me, and had quit and wanted the other people to be able to stop too. But just the opposite happened. I got back on after a while. So I just left the house to those people and went to Oakland to get my head together.

"In Oakland I got another job and called up Mike from there. He got a job where I was working. We were really good buddies. We'd been through a lot together. That's the time I got into the Hell's Angels. I kind of ran on the edges, but I had a bike. Ran around. I was working in a hospital again, but nothing solid had happened in my life, so I got back into drugs there too. Nothing gave me stability.

"I was dealing real heavy then, making $2000 a week, which I spent. I don't know what on. I just spent it. The funny thing was that when I really got heavy into dealing, I began getting away from it myself. You just can't do good business loaded. I saw that.

"That's when I met Nancy at a party. She worked in inhalation therapy too." He glances affectionately over at Nancy, who is wiping Aaron's cooing mouth. Then she helps him down to the floor. Nancy's face is set off by long yellow hair. Her smile is serene and her manner calm and pleasant. She nods her head in response to Del's reference.

"Yes, we were both in inhalation therapy. I had worked in hospitals and really enjoyed it, but in my work I saw a lot of death. And I was freaked out by the deaths around me. Del and I met at a time when we both were searching.

"After we met and got together, we both quit our jobs, just dropped out. Del let his hair grow and I did too. Then I got pregnant deliberately so that I could get on welfare and Del began dealing. I tried grass and pills, but I never really dug it. For a while I thought it might be an answer, but I never really got behind it. We were into a lot of heavy mind games, psyching people out. A lot spoken, not much said. We freaked people out by bluffing. You see, there wasn't much else. I knew I loved Del, and I felt he really cared for me. I think both of us had come to the point where we realized that there was either something or nothing.

"And that's just when Glenda Sue came to our house. We were living in a commune with six other people, and she had been one of the guy's girlfriends. She had left a while back, and we heard she was at some kind of Bible school in Ohio, but nothing more. It sounded pretty weird. She came suddenly and stayed for less than a week; and although I didn't like her personally because she was so heavy on the pressure, we did see that there was hope." Nancy pauses to call Aaron back from the swinging doors.

"Yes, we had known Glenda Sue before she went to Ohio, and we thought she was strange," Del emphasizes with a shake of his head. "When she returned, her mind was totally healed. She had a sound mind, and she began witnessing to her former boyfriend, but he never heard her.

"She told us about the 'Power for Abundant Living' Class, and right then we decided to take it. Two weeks after she left, we took the class in Alameda, and once we decided to take it, we just never wavered from the decision. That was in

October of 1969. It was a film class. We had no money at that time, and Mr. Yeremian loaned us the money.

"Nancy and I had already begun to read the Bible together, even before Glenda Sue came back, but we just couldn't understand it. I'd always believed in God ever since I was a child. I could never get into jokes about the Lord. I used to tell people that someday I'd be working full-time for God. Then I'd wonder why I'd said it. Back in LA, I met a girl in the hospital, a staunch Roman Catholic, and she really got me to think about and pray to God. I always prayed a lot, but I'd never let on to my friends that I prayed. I'd pray: 'Lord, show me how you want me to live.' I just knew there must be answers somewhere. And then every night of the class my mind was totally blown. I saw the truth and I accepted it. I knew it was truth.

"After we had the class, I went to talk to my friend Mike Martin. The day I went to see him he'd just prepared a fix that would have killed him. He'd had it with everything. Now he's branch leader on the Oakland side." Del laughs as the past comes back into mind. His eyes under pale yellow eyebrows are a straight-forward and honest blue. Nancy has freed Aaron from the swinging door to the kitchen, and they are back. She sits down, her stomach laying on her lap like an oversized basketball under her paisley printed red and blue blouse.

"It was something how things began to happen when we started the class," Nancy picks up. "Del began to get jobs. He was doing moving jobs with my brother, and they just got one job after another. That class really began to set us free — from fear especially.

"At the same time the situation in our house really deteriorated. The others started having wild orgies. More violence. We'd come back from the class and find things like 'Death is Good' written on the walls. None of the others in the house got turned on, and we knew we had to find another place.

"The change in our lives was really fantastic. Del got a steady job, so we had money coming in, and we began to look for a place. We were going to fellowships three evenings a week, and every day we'd check the papers, ask and hunt, but either the rent was too high or it was already gone by the time we got there.

"That's when we decided to call Dr. Wierwille and ask him what it was we were doing wrong. So I called him, and he was just tremendous. He said: 'Don't worry, there's a better house ready for you, just keep believing and keep looking.'

"It was a real shot in the arm. Every house we looked at after that got better and better. We knew we wanted a place with a room big enough to have fellowships, a room for the baby, and I wanted a fireplace.

"Not long after the phone call, we saw an ad in the paper. It was some special deal in an unlikely section, but we thought we'd go look at it anyway. We walked into a big room, really good-sized, and both of us knew that was it. I didn't see a fireplace, but I figured — oh well, everything else was just right. And then we walked into the second room. And there was a fireplace! Then we just knew it was the perfect place. It was beautifully laid out and the guy said: 'I don't know why I'm letting you have it. Someone else is really interested. But, it's yours.'

"That's when we really started growing and learning. We had fellowships two or three times a week and took turns teaching. We got to having thirty or forty people every time. That was in January." Nancy pauses and then breaks into a smile, as though she were getting to the really exciting part of the story. "And then Dr. Wierwille invited us to join the Way Corps."

"But that's a whole other long story," Del remarks, gathering together his dishes to take into the kitchen. "This ministry is something fantastic. People are rising up to believe now. God is ready to move the Word over the world if people don't blow it. I see Dr. Wierwille as the next man of God to rise up after Paul's death. It's taken that long to rise up in believing. This is no whim of my fancy. I've thought of this for months. Put things together. The only thing I can imagine is that the Lord is coming back soon and the Church is being gathered together. It's a great life. But we don't know when He's coming back, so I got some things to do today," he stands up in his casual manner, but I am reluctant to have him leave. I don't know when I will catch him again like this at breakfast — so ready to open his heart to me.

"What about the Corps?" I asked him quickly. "What do you think of the program and the training?"

He considers a few seconds before answering. "The Corps as a program is the best. To live here and have the Doctor work with us is extraordinary. He allows us to see the ministry through his eyes. He shares everything with us. And sometimes it's a bummer. But he lays it out.

"The idea of the Corps is to transmit the commitment and dedication of the ministry to us so that we can teach others where he can't be himself. It works by osmosis here. I can't quite express it in words, but I can feel it and see it and know it. It's learning to be keen and sensitive to the spirit of God anywhere and anytime. We are really privileged to be able to do this here.

"I'm not saying this is the only place it can be done. It's possible to reach that point of knowledge and zeal anywhere if people work the Word and renew their minds. But this, the Corps program, is the fastest way. What we learn here in two years would take ten to fifteen years in the outside world to learn." With a smile, he excuses himself, taking his dishes to the kitchen, and with a congenial "God bless you" over his shoulder, strides out the door.

"It's the best place in the world to be, and the greatest time to be alive," Nancy remarks, helping Aaron put on his little jacket. "Things are moving so fast in this ministry. The Doctor has had a vision for years of getting the Word out so everyone can hear it at least once and decide whether to believe it or not, but people have just not risen up and believed God 'til now.

"You were at the meeting last Sunday when he talked about the new way of presenting the Word to people. He is ready to go on a campaign for the next 18 months, one week a month in major cities all over the country, to teach God's Word and make the class available to anyone who wants it. I'm just so thankful I heard about the class and got turned around on to the right track. And I know there are lots of people hungry and searching who'll get blessed."

We talk a few more minutes and then Nancy leads Aaron out by the hand. The dining room is empty except for Debbie, who has already begun carrying the green and yellow pitchers to the washroom, and me. On the small clock over the counter, the hands point to a quarter 'til eight.

The dining room is not much to look at empty. The floors are gray concrete, the walls a creamy off-white. One wall is nearly covered by a huge airline map of the world, with green ribbons stretching from Ohio to every place where there is a fellowship. Like most of the things around here, the dominating theme is simplicity, neatness, and designed to serve its function best.

Sitting over my second cup of coffee, I recall my impressions when I arrived here for the first time last summer. When someone told me to go to the Biblical Research Center, I flashed on a mind picture: huge collections of dusty volumes, a deathly silence hanging in the air, interrupted now and then by the sharp turning of a page. I expected to find a scattering of individuals huddled in corners, poring over old books looking up obscure references. After all, all the research I had ever done throughout my years in college and graduate school, especially concerning something as old as the Bible, had been done in that manner. I expected red tape, cards to sign, forms to fill out, tiptoed footsteps and people admonishing me to be quiet and whisper. But I soon found that I was totally wrong.

The Biblical Research Center is the gathering point for fellowship and the source of feeding the Body. It is a place for people, not books, for God's portion is His people. And those who believe God's Word are to be living epistles to be read of all men. It is each individual studying, researching, believing and then acting on what God says that makes the Word living and real. The Biblical Research Center is a place of life and light, warmth and fellowship, a place to be used and enjoyed.

And like everything around here, this space is used efficiently. The building is L-shaped with two levels: the main floor above ground and the basement. One wing of the basement contains the dining room and kitchen where the cooks now are discussing aspects of today's menu. The long wing of the ell is basically one room, which can be subdivided by folding doors into three large cubicles along one side. On the far end a couch and several chairs make up a sitting area referred to as the student lounge. The ceilings of the basement are low and well lighted, so that I hardly notice that there are no windows.

Danny Shroyer wanders over and helps himself to a cup of coffee from the coffeemaker. Although he always looks casual and unhurried, he is here early for a day's work. At 26, with a heavy shock of gray hair and a very gentle, quiet manner, he is head of the Mailing and Receiving Department.

"God bless you, good morning," he greets the cooks and me in his particularly genial way and sips his coffee. From Ohio, Danny worked for years in a machine shop until he came here full-time last fall. Having taken the class as a teenager, he admits to having been through it over a dozen times. He is presently responsible for packing tapes, films, books and other materials and shipping them to every corner of the nation as well as abroad — a tremendous job to run efficiently. During most of the day the basement of the Biblical Research Center is his work area where he whistles as he packs, surrounded by packing boxes, masking tape and string. I ask him about his work today.

"Oh, today is a great day," he responds pleasantly. "I have eleven boxes to send to Kansas. I pack them here in the basement and UPS picks them up. But it's tricky, because they won't take more than 100 lbs. to any one address, so I have to pack things up in 100 pound loads and mail each package to a different address in Wichita.

"But that's nothing," he continues with a chuckle." The first week I started to work here I had to mail two hundred sets of the class materials to New York, California and Kansas. That was an order. But every week isn't like that. Last week there wasn't much mailing to be done, so I straightened up the storage area in the barn. You know that's our biggest storage area.

"There aren't many companies that do same-day filling of orders. But we do. We get an order in and mail it out that very day. The other side of my job is keeping an active inventory of all the supplies. I do a complete inventory in the barn

every two weeks. I know how many envelopes we have exactly. You think ten thousand or even thirty thousand lasts a
long time, but one mailing really eats into that.

"And I do all the deliveries here on the farm. I get the
packages in the morning and take them to the right department; then I deliver things between departments, like stuff
from Printing to Collating, and when it's been collated, to
Storage or here to Mailing, wherever it has to go.

"It'll be much better when we move the Print Shop over
to the Outreach House in town. That'll be sometime this
summer. Then I'll have a ramp. The Print Shop, Collating and
Storage will all be together and that will speed up operations.

"It's a great time. I'm getting all keyed for when the Doctor starts his teaching campaign. The numbers will really go
out then. But all I have to know is that we're going to make
it every day. If I think about the numbers, it's staggering.
But, I don't think about that, I just know it's going to work
out."

He finishes his coffee, takes his cup into the kitchen, and
ambles over to the student lounge. Cheerful and relaxed,
Danny hardly ever looks rushed, and yet accomplishes a
tremendous volume of work each day.

Linda Filbrun, a pretty blond Way Corps member, also
from Ohio, is just opening up the book storage room which is
near my table at one corner of the dining room. Upstairs, off
the main auditorium, is a small Bookstore where Dr. Wierwille's books, Way Productions records, Bibles and related

books are sold. Linda's responsibility throughout the week is to keep the Bookstore and books dusted, the Bookstore stocks replenished from this small storage closet and also to fill mail orders which come in daily. That is what she begins now, giving Danny the orders to mail out. With a pencil and pad in hand, she carefully counts the stocks, as she fills the orders.

There is a clattering of dishes from the dishwashing room, and a scraping and rattling of pots and pans from the kitchen. Nevertheless, I catch the strains of a radio's muffled blaring from the direction of the student lounge. That's Meg, the W.O.W. ambassador we met early this morning.

A prolific artist, she puts in a full day behind a long table in one corner of the basement, turning out one artwork after another. Her posters decorate the basement walls: the Word of God in cartoons, Snoopy soaring over the world on a huge Bible, a series of posters in Spanish for South America and, more recently, a series of posters for the outreach in Africa where the scriptures are translated into Loucazy and Lozi for people working in Zambia.

She's tapped into the pulse of the ministry, and whatever is happening oozes out of her very fingertips through paints, crayons, ink, magic markers or collage onto paper and goes up on the wall, wherever it's needed, for all to see. On Valentine's Day, there was a large heart on a huge white doily, emblazoned with: "Love All Year Around." Another day there was a series of Peter Max posters augmented by Bible verses.

"Peter Max is the best," she shared with me the day they came out, "but you can get terribly lost in his posters. You wander around aimlessly. There's nothing to hold on to. So I just put the Word of God in there. Your eye is drawn into the picture and then it stops on the Word. The Word gives order. When you're on the Word, you know exactly where you are."

I make my way to her cubicle now to say good morning. Both the folding doors are closed, but through the crack at one end I see her working diligently. She smiles frequently, laughs openly, chats as she works.

"What are you on today, Meg?" I ask her. She has before her a huge piece of white pasteboard fastened securely on her drawing board, and is gently carressing it in minute strokes with a thin, black pen.

"This is a poster for the Rock of Ages this summer in August. Did you go to the Rock of Ages last summer? There were over a thousand people there for most of the weekend, and almost five thousand on Saturday night. This year it's going to be even larger. They are expecting between five and fifteen thousand." She giggles, her eyes beaming as she speaks. "This poster is getting ready to be mass-produced either here or on the outside."

I comment on the delicate beauty of minute lines at opposing angles, which create a huge sunrise.

"Yes, it's coming along fine," Meg agrees, leaning her head back to catch the entire effect. "But I picked a slow medium for this one. It'll take a while. It's so great to be with God. Do you know, I never have a moment's head hassle or wonder? I never spend time worried or concerned, asking myself: What should I produce? How shall I make it? What will they think of it?

"I just get in here and say: 'Well, Father, what do you want me to do today?' And right then I get the clearest picture of the next thing to do. Did you see the record cover for Selah's new album? I finished it yesterday." She pulls out an album-size painting, a combination of Beardsley-Middle Eastern pattern of orange, tan and white leaves and flowers on a sky-blue background. Below in stately letters, SELAH, and above that in eye-arresting formal script the meaning of the Hebrew word which is the name of the album: 'Consider These Words.' It is a stunning display of discipline and artistry.

She smiles radiantly at my enthusiasm and starts talking about her next big project. There is no lingering with past success or failure, but rather: Well, what's next?

"I'm going to be doing a series of 300 posters for the Children's Fellowship. I'm working with Helene Richey, the teacher of the little ones. We're going to get all the principles of the 'Power for Abundant Living' Class down on huge posters for the kids, so that they can really grasp them visually. I'm really looking forward to that. It's going to be so much fun," and she pauses from her minute pen strokes long enough to utter a hearty chuckle of anticipation and throw me a kiss across her table.

"What were you doing before you got into the Word, Meg?" I ask her.

"I was strung out. Really strung out. It was like my head was separated from my body. I was just all doped up. Then I got into trouble after trouble, owed people money. I couldn't get it together. I was just like two people. I was working a job where I had to maintain a 'together' exterior — you know, straight and clean. I'd go home, wear a nice dress, talk sweet. But in my other life I was the heavy pusher, the most freaked out, creepy character you ever met.

"I knew I was going nowhere, but I kept thinking: ' There must be something.' But I just couldn't find it. I was completely severed from my body. I got to the point where I was in a hospital writhing on the bed, but I wasn't in pain. My mind was just standing above and beyond my body. I looked down at myself and I said: 'If that's Meg, I don't want any part of her. It's all bad.' And I was ready to turn my back on her and leave her there, writhing.

"I tried suicide, but somebody got to me before I could make it. Praise the Lord. There was just nothing to live for, nothing that counted. Or if there was, I couldn't find it." She looks up and smiles radiantly at me. "But God is good. He found me, and look where I am now." She waves her hand ecstatically, just as Barbara Fair slips in through the opening at the end of the folding door.

Barbara is in the Way Corps, and is part of the Art Department. Her long blonde hair falls almost to her waist and her stylishly mod taste in clothes makes her look more like New York than Wichita, Kansas, where she is from.

"People just come in here all the time," Meg continues in mock despair, looking up from her drawing board, "because I just can't close the door — ever, ever, ever." A wave of laughter washes over the room, and the radio throws in the staccato strains of 'Me and Julio Down by the School Yard.'

Barbara pulls out her drawing board to continue sketching a coloring book about Daniel and the lions. Meg continues her minute strokes of the pen, and the conversation meanders lazily from one topic to the next.

"Last night in the girls' trailer we had a pillow fight, the good old-fashioned kind."

"Yeah, the kind where Meg is the only one with a pillow."

"That was fun. Brenda said: 'Now wait, you guys, I'm going to sleep,' and then she ended up talking for 45 minutes with somebody. I didn't keep her awake with my pillow fight. She kept herself awake with her conversation."

The theme moves to eating, overeating and smoking, as both girls lean over their work in concentration.

"Isn't it amazing how long our bodies hold out considering all the stuff we do to them? Now that in itself is a miracle. God sure did a good job in forming them."

"Yeah, and to think they're only made of dust."

"Yeh, I've sure left a lot of tracks in the dust. I've used and abused my body all these years, really given it to it."

"So have I, boy. If my body could only talk, the stories it could tell," Meg finishes with an exaggerated moan that turns into laughter.

Becky and Gloria lean in the door to say good morning as they work at cleaning the Biblical Research Center, and it is time to see the children off to school.

Nick and Sylvia are already upstairs in the Biblical Research Center, just inside the canopied door, watching for the yellow bus to come down the road. John Paul and Sara, the Doctor's two youngest children, both in high school, are walking across the grass from the big house. The bus swings into the driveway, and with a blast of chill through the open door and a bunch of good-byes, the school children disappear for the day, carried off by the lumbering yellow vehicle. It makes a circle through the farm, stopping for the Randall boy, the two Allen girls, and in a few moments retreats down the road by which it came.

The sun is higher now, but the grayness of nebulous clouds has temporarily hidden it. A tinge of mist rises over the pond. The grounds are still. In spite of the over forty people who live and work here, there is almost no one to be seen.

Across the brown, crinkled ground from the barn, Sue Wilson is just returning from feeding the animals. That is her main responsibility here in the Way Corps. Formerly a horse trainer with her own riding school, she is currently in charge of feeding the livestock and training the horses. In her short leather jacket, worn bluejeans and silver wool beret, I catch her almost every morning about this time and again in the mid afternoon returning from the barn. A moment later, and she is gone.

From behind the barn, as every day, the tractor pulling a wooden wagon laden with large garbage barrels swings out through the driveway in this direction. Randy, the youngest man in the Way Corps, in his faded denim jumpsuit is out to collect the garbage from building to building. Today he seems to move especially quickly, speeding the tractor about. Mark, the red-bearded audio engineer from New York helps him. Bits of conversation fly through the air between them — broken one-liners, half-formed jokes and words of exhortation. It doesn't matter. They also simply do the job and enjoy the responsibility. Everything has to be done; all things must be carefully maintained to last as long as possible; see what needs to be done, and then do it heartily as unto the Lord and not unto men.

It may be the eve of spring, but the air is raw. I am glad to be back in the warmth of the entrance to the Biblical Research Center. The little hallway is paved in flagstones, but the main auditorium is carpeted in lively red. All the chairs in the main hall are of the folding variety, and for Sunday night meetings are set out in neat rows from the front to the back — the hall seats about 300. But this is midweek, and today the hall is empty, the chairs stacked carefully at the back so that Becky and Gloria have a clear field to clean.

Directly to the left as one enters the back of the hall, an inconspicuous door is slightly ajar. That is the sound room — Howie Yeremian's room. Right now, the rhythmic harmonies of "Traffic" reach my ears. This tips me off that Howie is there.

Sure enough, as I push open the door, he is seated in his tiny sound-proofed cubicle surrounded by a master tape deck with four tape recorders and duplicators, and other electronic equipment to the right and to the left that is a mystery to me. On the counter before him is one of the tape recorders, open, dismantled, surrounded by a variety of little pieces, one of which he is carefully regarding through the thick, black-rimmed glasses he always wears.

Howie is also in the Way Corps. At 25, he has had two years of electronics in college, training in an electronic factory and four years of experience in the field doing electronic work on a radio station in California where he lived before he came here.

His responsibility is the upkeep of all electronic sound equipment and video tape — that includes all the tape recorders, the PA sound system, amplification, tape duplication and in general anything electronic on the farm.

I ask him about the video equipment.

"We're still deciding what to do with it. The greatest profit has been during the W.O.W. ambassador training program. We'd video tape all the teachings, and then we could show them as they were originally given to other groups of ambassadors. It's also been great for us in the Corps. When we teach and it's video taped, we can go back and analyze our teaching techniques and improve.

"We got all the video tape equipment the middle of last summer, and we've had some problems in modifying the units so they work together perfectly. We've taped one Advanced Class so far. Since we got the equipment we've taped about a hundred reels that are stored here and in the barn. We tape all the Sunday night teachings here, but I still don't know exactly which way we're going with it. We may change eventually from 16mm film to doing the Foundational Class in color video.

"We have three film projectors here on the farm, which I take care of too, but 16mm can go through 15-20 runs before it begins scratching, while the video tape can go through 80 before it begins to wear out. Right now, the equipment is just right. We'll have to see how things work out in the future. When there are a whole lot of classes going, more than now, we'll see what the best way is."

Howie leans over the small recorder part he's refitting. He has a black beard on his chin and black side burns. With his rapidly receding hairline, he has the look of a patriarch from ancient days. His face radiates a gentleness, a kindness, far more impressive than his large frame and tall stature.

In his cubicle, he is surrounded by cut-outs from magazines, a poster by Meg and one beautiful, colored reproduction of the Golden Gate Bridge in San Francisco, where he came from. There is not much wall space between his machines so several pictures are hung on the ceiling. As official photographer for the headquarters, Howie has several of his snapshots pinned in one cluster. It is a cozy space to work in.

It is easy to fall into conversation with Howie as he works. The "Traffic" tape terminates, and he puts on another favorite, "Chicago." There's a buzz on the intercom. Debbie downstairs wants to know if Howie would please switch the music on in the kitchen so that they can have some rhythm to clean up to. Howie adjusts several buttons and switches on the PA system.

"How did you hear about this place?" I ask him.

"I'm from California. Before I heard of The Way I was already involved in a Christian youth radio station. It was kind of Class B, a small station; all kinds of second-class rejects from the big radio stations worked there. I was an audio-engineer on that station then.

"I was also attending Bible College because I had problems, and everybody said: 'If you have problems, go to Bible College.' So I went. But I didn't dig it much. It was dull.

"Everyday I'd commute to work by car to the smart sayings of Steve O'Shea, the famous Rock Jock. Between Bible College and the second-rate radio station, he was the exciting high point of my day. He was great, real funny and clever, the brightest thing happening in my life. That was in 1967, winter.

"Then one day I got to work and there was excitement all around. Steve O'Shea had been saved. He'd found Christ, and our station had a tape of his testimony. We must have listened to it a half-dozen times that night.

"Steve O'Shea, that was his radio name, is really Steve Heefner, the limb leader of the Way East now. He got involved in a Christian house in Haight-Ashbury, and I started going there. I just cut classes and spent time there. I could see that something was really happening, much more than in my church group or even in the Bible College.

"I started sending people over there or asking Steve to my house and then inviting young people over to meet him, and let him talk to them himself.

"That winter Dr. Wierwille came to see Steve. I guess either Steve or his wife, Sandi, could tell you more about that. All I saw was that it made a great impression on Steve. 'He said a lot of good things,' Steve told me. That was all, but it was very rare for Steve to say that about anybody, there was so much inter-denominational fighting among the groups he was involved in. But he was really searching for the true Word.

"That summer Steve and Sandi came here to the farm. They were coming for just two weeks to see what was happening and to set the people here straight. That's what they said at any rate, when they left.

"After a couple of weeks, I would stop by the station to see if he was back yet. But the people over there just kept shaking their heads.

"At the very end of summer, one day I was walking by and there was Steve threading up a tape recorder. I was real glad to see him and went in to rap for a while. I remember the conversation very well. I told him how I'd just met some Jehovah's Witnesses and had written for them a three-page analysis proving for sure that there was a Trinity. Steve just listened all the time and went on with what he was doing. Then he said something like: 'You know, when you get deeper into it, you might find that Jesus and God are not quite the same thing, and that God and the holy spirit may be more similar than it looks like at first.' That was it. He just kept on working. He didn't argue or try to prove anything to me.

"He really impressed me. He seemed much calmer, more together and much more sure of himself. I kept hanging in with him, and he told me about the class. I kept listening and then I decided I'd try and take the class myself.

"That was right after Christmas. I thought my father would refuse to let me go. It was all kind of sudden, and I had some other commitments. But when I approached him, he said: 'Sure, go ahead.' So I flew out in January 1968 and took the 'Power for Abundant Living' Class here at the farm.

"When I came back to California, I knew that was it. I left Bible College and did more and more with the Word. After that things really began moving in California. Reverend David Anderson came out and ran some film classes. That was where I first met Del and Nancy Duncan. They had come from a real heavy scene. But then, most of the people in the classes had.

"Things began to grow so fast — classes, twig fellowships, new people, and more of each. Then my sister, Cathi, took the class, and then my mother and finally my father. Now Cathi and I are both here in the Corps. We're the only brother and sister in this Corps. It's been a fantastic year, more than I ever could have imagined it to be. That's how much I'm getting out of it."

The intercom buzzes him again. He exchanges a few words and rises from his swivel chair.

"I have to go to Cincinnati to pick up some parts now. God bless you. See you later." With one motion scooping up his jacket, he is out of the door.

On the other end of the main auditorium, through a door behind the speaker's platform is the Printing Department. I make my way over there now to pick up another year of back issues of *The Way* magazine to look over.

J. Fred Wilson runs the Printing Department. Sitting behind his desk which protrudes halfway into the room, he is the picture of business elegance. Short black hair, with sideburns, a neat mustache, mod-flavored tie with colors from a psychedelic sundae, and lavender shirt, Fred worked for many years in advertising and public relations before joining the staff here two years ago. Like many of the staffers, he, his wife and three children live in town, and he often commutes on his motorcycle. He looks up from his work, greeting me with a smile.

"How about a year of old magazines starting in 1955?" I propose, having to shout slightly over the rumbling of the printing press which Tina, a Way Corps girl, is overseeing in the corner. I note that she is running off copies of the Jonah coloring book, just completed by Meg. A strong odor of chemicals fills the room. Lonnell Johnson, the oldest Way Corps member, nearing thirty, is burning plates in another corner of the room, but no one there seems to give the smell any notice. On Fred's desk an assortment of dummies is spread out that he has been working for the next *Way Magazine*.

The Print Shop is a one-room operation. A second room behind this one doubles as a dark room and storage area, where the high shelves are neatly stacked with reams of many varieties of paper.

"You've got quite an operation here," I remark, as Fred hands me the green box marked "Way Magazine, 1955-57."

"Oh yes, we print everything for The Way: registration cards for the classes, the magazine, bulletins, books, pamphlets, letters, brochures, forms, anything that comes up.

"Two years ago we had one hard-cover book in print, but now we have six out, and the printing volume has quadrupled in two years. When I got here, this was a thimble-sized operation, but now it's a heavy load for six to eight people. Things really began mushrooming when the young people started flocking in after 1969."

"It's a pretty tight operation, too," I respond in understatement.

"Yes," Fred agrees, sitting back and folding his hands behind his head. "There is someone on the press all day. Meg and Barbara do art work for me. Lonnell has enough to keep him busy. I've found that everyone does better if they are involved with more of the process, less specialization. It's best to let each person do a job through. That way they enjoy it more, having more of a feeling of accomplishment, and get more understanding of the entire operation. So we rotate around — the press, layout, strip-in, burning plates, proof-reading — whatever has to be done.

"Howie does most of the photography. Sue Wilson and Nancy Bowen are available to help me when we have a heavy schedule. And Brian Heaney is here when Tina isn't.

"November and December were real heavy times. And May will be too. That's when we are getting ready for Summer School. All the collating is done in Trailer 8, and from there everything we don't need right away goes into the barn. Danny does all the moving."

He nods again. "Yes, it's a tight operation, but things work out when we need them. In December, just before Christmas, I mentioned to all the people in the Printing Department that we needed a light table and a new platemaker. We started lifting our needs to Father. It kind of got our thinking moving in that direction.

"Within a few days, a graphic arts salesman came with brochures for a light table, and we got just the one we needed. Then the day after that Howard Allen went to see a junk dealer in Columbus and he had the exact platemaker we needed for ten percent of the price of the new one. It was in excellent shape, really nice and just like new.

"It's like that with people. When we need extra people to work on things, they come along just at the right time." Fred chuckles as though tickled by the thought. "But we'll really have a smooth operation when we move the Print Shop to the Outreach House in town this summer. There'll be a lot more space for new volume equipment, and collating, mailing and storage will be all together. It'll be much more efficient."

I comment on the Christmas issue of the magazine, a silver dove on a sky-blue background, a sleek cover by Meg.

"It's a good magazine," Fred agrees. "No ads, just truth. The articles are always straight from the Word, good solid teachings. There's not as much art work and photography as I'd like, but it's coming. There's some news from various areas and some letters and sharing, but mostly it's the Word. You can't go wrong with that."

I nod in agreement to the rumbling of the press. It stops suddenly and the room is amazingly still. Tina refills the ink tank and puts in a fresh ream of paper, after piling the finished pages on a rack of shelves specially designed for collating in order.

"Well, thanks a lot for the magazines. It's been great talking with you," I call into the sudden stillness, and then I leave closing the screen door behind me. I'm not down the three steps to the paved path before I hear the rhythmic chung-chung-chung of the press begin again.

Along the road to the new office building Mrs. Wierwille is pedaling her bicycle, a package squeezed under her left arm.

Several people here, having many errands to run from one end of the farm to another, resort to bicycles.

By the red brick path to Trailer 5, George Jess is carefully pruning the young apple and plum trees. It is that time of year to prepare for the coming spring. Already the branches are growing lumpy, expectant with buds. God gives a man the opportunity to be steward of the land. Take care of what God gives you and He'll give it back to you increased. Man works the land with joy and in fellowship.

Inside Trailer 5 stillness reigns but for the twittering of the birds outside. Gary Curtis, a second-year Way Corps member, works here translating the class and other research into Spanish. Formerly a teacher of Spanish who spent time in Mexico and Spain, Gary is interested not only in Spanish translations, but also in seeing materials translated into French and German soon, as well as other languages later.

With his Spanish and English Bibles side by side on the desk before him, today he is working on the accurate translations of certain scriptures. Yesterday, Juan, a student from Bolivia, worked with Gary, recording parts of the class in Spanish on tape. But most of the time Gary works alone, with quiet self-discipline and great internal drive day after day to get the job done — so characteristic of the people in the Way Corps.

I lay the box of old *Way* magazines on my own desk. Unwilling to disturb Gary's concentration, I slip out of Trailer 5 again. By this time George Jess, with the help of Chris, the curly-haired Dutchman here as a special student, is already loading the pruned twigs into the truck. They are clearing the grass, keeping it clean for the day when it will turn green.

For all that is happening here, the grounds are definitely not bustling with activity. But that is because the main work being done here is spiritual, as each person lets God triumph in his mind all through the day.

The Main Office of The Way International looks no different from the other half-dozen mobile homes which populate the grounds. Outside the main door on a slender post, a modest sign reading: "H. E. Wierwille, Secretary-Treasurer," swings on its hinges blown by the wind. This trailer was once a dormitory, but now houses the bulk of administrative work. Let me take you there.

Inside the screen door, a large blackboard directs us to see Claudettee before going farther. On one wall of this tiny entranceway, mail baskets are marked with the names of people here at Headquarters. As I walk in, I nearly bump into Donna Randall who is just picking up the morning mail to take to Dr. Wierwille.

The wife of Gene Randall, the farm manager, Donna has a variety of responsibilities here. Having taken the class in 1960, she specializes in research. As an able teacher, she conducts a class in "Keys to Research." She brings in the morning mail and also handles special projects, such as editing and proofreading manuscripts for the Doctor. She plays piano at Children's Fellowship on Sunday nights, and as a matter of fact, she drove the school bus that came to whisk away the children early this morning.

Since moving here in 1966, she has worked on the magazine, printed, researched and collated, among other things. Like so many people here, Donna has done what needed to be done when it needed to be done.

Now she smiles in greeting to me, and holding the stack of mail in both hands walks quickly out the door in the direction of the Doctor's office.

Staccato office sounds enliven the main room where three typists are typing on a variety of machines. The sweet smell of apple blossom incense perfumes the air, and a radio plays the latest hits from behind Claudettee's desk.

Looking behind the standing blackboard which separates the entranceway from the main room, I see Claudettee, Brenda and Tricia working diligently, but not too busy to look up and smile. There is a little space to walk between the desks, but Velma Stork bustles through in my direction with a peel of cheerful laughter. The mother of four children (ages 28, 26, 23 and 16), Velma is in charge of the office work here.

"I used to do all the typing myself," she relates exuberantly; then waving her hand about the close quarters, she continues in answer to my comments, "but now I have girls to help me — three work a full eight-hour day, and Terry from the Way Corps, works here four hours a day. I know how to run all the machines, but now the girls do too. I oversee the tape duplicating machines and I am in charge of the tape library. Have you seen it? It is behind one wall in the Biblical Research Center, floor to ceiling. No one ever notices that it's a closet."

I hadn't realized the extent of her responsibilities, and we fall into conversation about how she got into the ministry.

"I heard of this place back in 1961, when there was an open house here. You see, we live in the local community. That's how I heard about the class. My husband and I took it. I started working here a little at a time, but it just grew and grew, and now I'm full-time.

"When I think back, there isn't much here I haven't done. I ran the kids' camp one summer. That was fun. I think back to the children — their believing is just so great. They don't have a whole lot to unlearn.

"One summer, when Dr. Williams was here from India, we read in the papers that they were going to move all the people out of Bombay because of a terrible water shortage. Our little kids in the camp were four to twelve years old, and they decided to pray for water over there. Right after that, the rains came. Afterward we learned that it happened the same day and hour that we prayed for them. It was a miracle, but I wasn't surprised. When you believe God, you just expect things to happen.

"But you want to know something about the office, I bet. That's a miracle too, the work we do here. The strength and health to do it is a miracle. And whenever we need help, it arrives just as we need it. When we expand, the right person comes in with the right skills.

"I used to do all the typing myself until this fall. I'd type letters, and all the books on the MTST machine. I spent a solid week typing up the "Power for Abundant Living" book a year ago February. I'd get up at 4 AM every morning and type until midnight, just taking off time to eat meals.

"The MTST is a Selectric tape composing machine. It types manuscripts onto tape and automatically puts them into even columns. Then we take a picture, make a negative and burn metal plates from the negative. The plates go on the offset printing press, and then we run off copies. All except the typing part is done over in the Printing Department.

"But that's why we have so much typing to do here. We handle everyone's correspondence, type their work and do the magazines and books here too."

Velma breaks off her narrative as Brenda, a staff member from Washington, D.C., joins us with a hospitable smile.

"Can I get you some coffee?" she offers me.

I decline.

"Look at Brenda," Velma continues, regarding Brenda affectionately, "do you know that when she came here, she just knew the typewriter? Then I showed her the Executive typewriter, and now she knows the Composer and the MTST.

"And to think, I used to think a typewriter was a typewriter," Brenda laughs. "We don't mind the work. Everyone just enjoys it so much. Look here in this little office. And I mean little," Brenda emphasizes. "I'm from D.C., Claudettee is from Wichita, Tricia is from Rochester, New York, and we are all working together to get the Word out. It's great." Brenda returns to her typing, as Velma and I take a few steps through the long, narrow room.

"We're all a happy bunch of nuts," Velma chuckles. "With nuts, the goodies are on the inside, not on the outside."

"But typing is not all that you do here. What is that over there?" I ask pointing to a long piece of technical equipment which Charlene is running.

"Oh, that's for film cleaning. The films from the film classes go out from here, and when they come back, they have to be cleaned. That's Charlene's job, along with other things. She works with Reverend David Anderson. He is in charge of all the classes — tape and film. They go out through him. We have eight sets of the Foundational class on film and 52 sets of the tape classes. That's all done here. Dave can tell you more about that. He's in the back there.

"We do all the tape duplicating here too. I'll show you." Velma leads me back among the desks to the entranceway and down a tiny corridor. The trailer is set up as a private home, two small bedrooms off the corridor, an efficiency kitchen, where coffee is perking, a dining area, now all occupied by office staff, all in addition to the long room where the typing pool sits.

The smallest bedroom off the corridor, barely large enough for two people to sit in, houses the tape duplicating equipment. Sunny Sanders, a Way Corps member from California, is in here working, surrounded by stacks of tapes and tape boxes. Tall, long-legged, beautiful, with a delicately featured oval face surrounded by waves of long black hair, she looks like a model who just walked off the cover of a fashion magazine.

"We can do three blank copies at a time," Velma explains pointing to a small machine. "We put the original in front here, and the blanks beside it. The 1200-foot tapes take eight minutes, and the 1800-foot tapes take twelve minutes."

"Monday is our big day in here, after the Sunday night meeting," Sunny adds. "We start duplicating the Sunday night teaching and it goes out to over 100 people every week. By Tuesday morning we have them all packaged, labeled and mailed out. They go to the limbs, branches, twigs and individuals who want to keep up with what's happening in the ministry.

"Besides that, people write in and order taped teachings from our catalog. We duplicate them here and send them out. Some people send the tapes back so that we can erase them and put something else on them."

As the tape duplicator whirrs, Sunny is putting red leaders on a bunch of new tapes.

"Do you do it all yourself?" I ask her.

"Mostly, but on the heavy days Terry or Naomi Bliss or Nancy Duncan comes in to help out."

"We have to keep operations fluid by checking the time it takes to do a job. With all the growth we're getting, it's turning into big business," Velma relates excitedly. Excusing herself, she returns to her desk. I wander back through the neat little kitchen to the dining area, now serving as the "executive" offices of The Way.

You might not catch that at first glance — "the executive offices." In the square area, three desks are neatly compressed together, one against each of the three walls, having barely enough room for the three men to sit back to back, each overseeing his area of responsibility.

You may think the space is tight, that people are constantly stepping on each other's toes, losing important papers in the shuffle and getting into each other's hair. But let me ask you this: How much room does a mind picture occupy? How much space does a decision take? How many shelves and drawers does one need to keep a clear plan of a day's work, or a week's work or a year's project?

The space might seem small, but the minds that work here are unfettered. At one desk, H. E. Wierwille, affectionately called "Uncle Harry" by nearly everyone, handles all the books and finances with Velma's occasional help.

At the second desk, Howard Allen, the general manager, handles the smooth running of the entire Headquarters: maintenance, allocation of labor, guests, transportation, delegating work to be done, so that there are no bottlenecks and everything is available and working when needed.

At the third desk, Reverend David Anderson, the youngest of the three men, in his late twenties, is responsible for all classes around the country, both film and tape. When enough people are together to form a class, he is the one who sees to it they have all materials promptly, and that a capable believer runs the class. He also teaches others to run classes effectively and smoothly.

This morning, Howard's chair is empty, which is not in the least surprising, as he is constantly moving from one corner of the farm to another overseeing the progress and the needs. But Uncle Harry is at his desk poring over long lists of figures, while Dave, at his desk a few feet away, is plugged into a tape, completely absorbed in the information seeping into his ear from the tiny earphones.

I always enjoy talking with Uncle Harry. Full of earthy wisdom, terse in his use of words, direct in his gaze and ready to laugh, he is Dr. Wierwille's older brother. At 65, he often states that he doesn't have an ache or a pain in his whole body. A successful businessman in the upholstery trade, he has been a mainstay of support for this ministry over the years, coming in one or two days a week and on weekends to do the bookkeeping. As soon as he retires this July he will be on staff full-time.

I question him about the financial growth of the ministry over the years. He runs his hand through a heavy head of salt and pepper hair, and after a few seconds answers me in his rough-hewn voice.

"The first year here, we had an income of $230 or $240, I can't remember exactly. In 1971, the first year of the ministry in one state, that state by itself had an income of $144,000.

"At the Men's Advance a few weeks ago, we made a bid for $150,000 for our building plans. We need a new dorm, new facilities for all the people who want to come here. We got $3000. So we just returned the money to the people. We told them we can't build on this. We just gave it back. I believe someone will come along and meet our needs. This is not a ministry that goes out to beg and plead.

"Most people are selfish, just think of themselves; but giving is in all phases: time and money. You have to help someone else to pull yourself out.

"I remember our first substantial gift very well. It was in 1959, in Florida. My brother Vic was down there teaching a class in Fort Myers. He was teaching without charge and we had expenses — transportation, room rental, our food, books and materials. I flew out there the last few days, and by then we were $1000 behind in our expenses.

"Well, we just believed God to meet our needs, and the last day an old lady came up and said she was clearing out her special savings account that she had put away in case of sickness. She said that now since she had taken the class she didn't need that anymore. She was real grateful and made out a check for exactly $1000. That is my first remembrance of a generous-sized gift." Uncle Harry pauses, swinging his swivel chair around to face me squarely.

"What really floated the ministry was good credit at the local bank. We would borrow and believe to get money for certain projects. It always came through. God's still in business. A few years ago, a banker in Troy first started the five-year trustee notes. That gave us operating capital at 6% per annum. With notes we could float $100,000.

"We just walk everyday, believe God and are thankful and enjoy life." I listen with intense interest. Uncle Harry rumbles when he laughs. I change the subject to his childhood, the family and how they grew up.

"Our grandmother came over from Germany around 1850 because of the military conscription there. My grandfather came about the same time too. Dozens of couples bought a boat and landed in New Orleans. There they bought a team of oxen. When they got here, they stopped — anchored.

"Our grandmother died in 1920. She died at 83, and two weeks before she died, she was hitching up her own horse. She gave each child a deed to a farm when they got married. She was a dynamo. VP got his energy from her.

"Our father was the youngest of seven children. He wanted an education, but Grandma said no. The tradition was that the youngest son stayed home and took over the farm. So that's what he did.

"Grandma made her money by selling eggs and butter in Cleveland. She culled them, put them in boxes and put them on the train to Cleveland, and sold them there for a quarter a box when all you could get around here was a few cents. She did the same thing with cream. Grandma was fearless. Sometimes people drove up to rob her because they knew she kept her money at home, but she'd just yell out the window and they would disappear. She was without fear.

"Grandpa died early, at about 45, but Grandma had a lot of life in her, lived almost twice as long. She lived here on this farm with our mother and father till 1920 when she died. She led the family devotions every morning. I remember that.

"Our father and mother had six children. Otto was the oldest boy. He was born in 1900 and killed in a car accident in Lima in 1930. It was a Sunday afternoon. He was driving a Ford coupe with his wife and son, Charles. A young guy was intoxicated, driving on the wrong side of the street. The impact threw the whole family out of the car and onto the streetcar tracks. He died of a brain concussion that very night.

"The wife and son sustained minor injuries. She remarried three years later, lives near here and Charles Wierwille is one of the head officers of the American Budget Company in New Bremen.

"The rest of us are still hearty. All live around here: Sister Lydia, you see her here almost every Sunday night, Sister

Sevilla — she lives over the other side of town, and Brother Reuben has the farm the back side of this one.

"VP was the youngest of us. He's ten years younger than me, and nearly twenty years younger than Lydie. The funny thing was no one in the house knew Mother was going to have a baby. We never even noticed — everyone busy — until the time he arrived. VP was a sickly child. Father's and Mother's upbringing was that the child should be baptized. We call it being "sprinkled" in the German Reformed Church. Because the child was so frail, they didn't wait five or six weeks as they usually did. They called the pastor early to come over and sprinkle him. And from that very hour, he was a different child.

"I didn't see much of him when he was growing up. When I was seventeen, I started to work, was away from home most of the time. That's near about when he started school. We all walked a mile to the same red schoolhouse. We all had chores to do: milking, feeding the cows, horses, hogs and sheep.

"Dad was a prosperous farmer in this area. We sold milk, eggs and hogs. We enjoyed life, lived well, but we never threw anything away. We had our own garden too. The only things we bought in the store were sugar and coffee. And everytime the parents went to town — which wasn't very often — they brought back a nickel's worth of candy for the children. A nickel bought a lot in those days.

"When VP was in high school, Dad wanted him to take over the farm later. You see, that was the tradition — that the youngest son take over the farm, just as he had done. But VP emphatically said no. He'd always liked to study and said he wanted to study for the ministry. Our Dad said, 'You haven't even learned to work well on the farm. You'll never make a good preacher.' But VP used to practice by preaching to the trees," Uncle Harry chuckles at the recollection. "He'd go out to the woods for hours. Dad thought he was loafing, but I knew what was going on. He was preaching to the trees.

"Our mother encouraged Dad to send the boy to seminary. He was always full of pep and vinegar. But he never hurt a soul. He did a few boy's tricks though, I guess. He played basketball, was always very energetic. That drive and desire for an education VP had is inherited. It came from his grandmother on our father's side. Even three years before he was ordained, he was preaching. In 1941, when he headed the church in Payne, Ohio, Dad and I went to hear his trial sermons. That was his first church — Payne, Ohio.

"Our mother died in January, 1941, and VP was ordained in June of the same year. Mom never lived to see him ordained. Our father married Emma in 1945. Funny, both his wives had the same first name. VP married them in 1945, and they lived here on this farm together. Dad died in June of 1956, and Emma lived here a few years. She died in 1967.

"Dad's will was that this home estate of 147 acres should go to Reuben, Victor, myself and Charles, our nephew, the son of Otto, while the two sisters, Lydie and Sevilla inherited an 80-acre farm north of St. Marys. In the transaction of the legal settlement of the estate in January, 1957, VP and I paid cash to Reuben and Charles for their shares. Then we, VP and I, bypassed ownership and put the deed directly in the name of The Way, Incorporated. We took the name from the book of Acts where people who believed were called followers of 'that way.'

"Yep, Doctor likes it here. It's home. Home is where you can take your shoes off. We moved here in 1961, February, a blusterous cold day." Uncle Harry shifts his weight in his chair, looking at me through his eye-glasses. With his white beard, mustache, his ruddy face, I suddenly think of a childhood memory of Santa Claus — someone radiating goodness and good cheer.

"VP could tell you about his life. I don't know much, had my own business, lots of work to do. I know one thing, though — VP always likes things done right, done the way they should be done. That's why at the Sunday night service everything is checked right up to snuff. See? Perfect. But that's the way we were brought up years ago. Our German people were not afraid of work. I guess that stays with you.

"After Payne, Ohio, he moved to Van Wert in 1944. That's where he had the church till he resigned in 1957. He was a good and active preacher, built a sermon well, got young people interested. But the inner depths of what he teaches now, I didn't know anything about it. If he was searching, I didn't know it. I was proud to have a minister in the family. Our closeness began back in Payne, and I always encouraged him to keep believing and backed him up in every way.

"The in-depth teaching really got going in 1957 when he resigned from the organized church. It wasn't a surprise, but then really it was. To branch away on your own like that is quite an undertaking. He had classes; he needed freedom, time to work the Word. And he had a family of five children to support. It was a real step of believing on his part.

"When he left the church, he took Rhoda with him. (She has the office down the hall, you know.) She had been the church secretary. That was a big expense. We undertook to believe for the support we needed to set him up. I became vitally interested then in his work. I wanted him to succeed in his venture. And if it was the Bible, it had to be true. He and I both thought he should try to reach church people. He wanted to go to church Sunday mornings. He really missed preaching. Early Sunday morning, like a race horse, VP was ready to go. He tried to go to churches, hoping to get spiritual food, but there was none.

"There are still many people who don't believe there's any more than the organized church offers. They're just not hungry or looking. And when he announced in January of 1960, in Troy, Ohio, that the Headquarters would be here in New Knoxville, his support was so thin that I had to pay Rhoda $30 a week out of my pocket. Very few had really seen the truth. They were all still playing church for an hour on Sunday mornings. Oh, they loved him. They all wanted him to eat their chicken and drink their coffee, but they didn't want to support his ministry.

"Well, things are changing now. People are starting to believe and walk out on it. When we first built the original part of the Biblical Research Center, I never thought we'd get it filled. But now on Sunday nights we have the auditorium full, and the overflow crowd of 50 or 100 are down in the basement watching the meeting on closed-circuit TV. And it's going to get bigger. This ministry gets people born again, and then teaches them the accuracy of the Word of God so they can live the more abundant life. But this is only the beginning. We haven't seen anything yet." Uncle Harry chuckles with quiet certainty, and muses to himself, "It wouldn't surprise me if I got a check for a million dollars today."

As Uncle Harry concludes, Dave Anderson unplugs the earphone from his ear and slapping his knee emphatically, swivels around to face us. Blond, energetic, he is a mechanical engineer by profession, but now full-time with The Way.

"That was a pretty good tape. I learned a lot this morning," he remarks, making occasional quick gestures with his hand. Uncle Harry's phone rings. He glides around 180 degrees to answer it, and I ask Dave about his department.

"What's happening here today? Tell me about the Tape and Film Department." I begin.

"It's fantastic," Dave asserts with enthusiastic confidence. "The tape library now has 540 tapes. This represents years of research. Now the research is on tape and it is available. Last year we sent out 70 to 100 tapes per week, about 5000 for the year. The growth has been in a geometric progression.

"In 1969, 380 people went through the Power for Abundant Living Class. In 1970, it was 760 people and in 1971, 2100 took the class. Last year new areas really opened up: Indiana, Minnesota, West Virginia, Colorado, Washington,

Alaska, Florida and Illinois, among other places. And work is beginning in eleven other states.

"When I compare this to 1968, I believe we can get the Word over the world in two years and three months. That's how long it took the Apostle Paul to get the Word out through all of Asia Minor, and he didn't have newspapers, TV or radio."

"I hear you had something to do with the film." I introduce a topic I had wanted to hear more details about.

"Yes, that was back in 1967. I had finished at Rutgers University and had gone to work in Cleveland. I'd already taken the class, and the more I saw it working, the more I believed. I was skeptical at first, had a lot of reservations. But I came to the point there in Cleveland where I decided I'd have fellowships once a week, even if nobody came.

"The first week my parents came. The second week aunts and uncles. And in a few weeks we had twenty people who wanted to take the class.

"I told the Doctor and he gave me some tapes. That's when he told me about the old films he had too. 'Try them out,' he said. They were black and white clips from the TV program called 'The Teacher' that he had made out of Lima in 1963.

"I was all set for a class. On the appointed day, out of twenty people who vowed they were interested, four showed up. I was furious. I was mad. I have never gotten teed off like that since then. But I learned a lot from that. After that, I never looked at numbers again. God said He'd do the adding. We just hold forth the Word. If people didn't come, they were the losers, not me. That was a real good lesson for me.

"The day I was going to show those films, Bob Wierwille blew into town. He's Doctor's nephew, Reuben's son. He's up in Alaska now, doing work for the ministry.

"Anyway, we showed the films that night and both of us saw right away that it was an effective way of teaching. After all, Doctor couldn't be in a lot of places at the same time. The films were good because neither Bob nor I had the authority to teach the Word with twenty-five years of research behind us.

"We both got really turned on to the idea of putting the whole class on film. Up until then, Doctor had to go everywhere to teach the class, although there were a few people who had enough experience to teach it effectively besides him. Rev. Mal George was one of them. We saw the film as a fantastic way to teach the class without Doctor having to be there everytime.

"The next Sunday we met with VP to talk about filming the whole class. We discussed what we needed, prices, color, people. By May of 1967, the plans were really moving along. We started to get bids — someone offered to do it for two and a half million bucks. We checked out more prices and figured that it would cost about a quarter of a million.

"But finally we had a breakthrough. Doctor got a price from Max Kent in Dayton to do it for $30,000. Now, that was a figure we could realistically imagine getting together. After that Bob and I traveled around the state to raise the money. In one night we raised $20,000. Everyone at one meeting gave one or two thousand. And Doctor raised the final $11,000 himself.

"That was my biggest contribution to the film, I guess, getting it started. After that, I went back to work in Cleveland, and I didn't get all the way involved in the production except for coming down to visit on weekends.

"VP really prepared for that film. He did more teaching than in any class previously. He went over his notes, studied and just lived it for two months before the filming began. He really got into it. They shot it that fall in two and a half weeks.

"VP taught three to six hours a day in half-hour segments. Then he'd stop, change his clothes — he'd be soaked through with sweat from the heat of the lights. His wife would freshen up the makeup and he'd go on again. There was one camera, and VP was on camera for 36 hours. There were no retakes.

"Wait a minute, there was one retake. He had gotten into it and then he just stopped. It had been a false start. So he just started again and we shot it again.

"We had the finished film in our hands in August of 1968. That's when we started the first film classes. We had from two to two dozen students in each class, but we should have started with a higher minimum because of wear and tear on the film. The charge was $20.

"First we said four to a class. In January of 1969, we did a class of 175 for free. But that was no good. We just got conned right and left because people kept coming, quitting and not really listening. They simply weren't committed to hear the whole teaching, so they kept copping out.

"We did free classes here in Ohio too, then in Florida. It took us a while to learn we were just burning ourselves out for nothing. We wanted to make it available. The film had already been paid for. But we've learned that people have to commit themselves, make an investment, to get something out of it. You've got to give to get. Ever heard that? It's in the Word. The law of giving — and people that didn't give anything, didn't get anything out of it, so it just wore out the film.

"Now we charge $65 for the film class including all the materials — a syllabus and four hard-bound books. You have to have eight signed up for a tape class and at least twenty for a film class. We don't like to have more than 44 in a film class either. That's a good number to handle.

"Well, what else do you want to know about the classes?" he inquires. I respond that I've learned a lot for one day. Howard strides in and I get up to give him back his chair. Velma bustles in to go over some more figures with Uncle Harry. There's a phone call for Dave. Howard is on the intercom checking with the garage to see if the Oldsmobile has been repaired and can go to Columbus in ten minutes. The typewriters are humming in a strident clatter in the adjacent room. Claudettee's radio is singing an old Beatle's hit: "It's just another day." Charlene at the film cleaning machine is humming along to herself. A burst of laughter from Claudettee spices the atmosphere. The door slams lightly. A few seconds later, slams again. People going in and out. Everyone working, everyone with a distinct purpose. Everyone together.

Well, that's it. It's just another day here in the executive offices of The Way International. It's just another day — everybody bubbling over from the inside, pouring it out in accomplishment. It's the family working together, doing what has to be done. How many families have you ever seen working together like this in warmth and cooperation over a long haul? I cannot think of one.

"It sure will be great to move into the new office building," Velma remarks as she accompanies me down the hall. "We will be moving next week, as soon as they finish laying the carpet in the new office building. Have you been over there yet? It sure is nice. We'll have a lot more space there. This is great. I'm glad we have had this whole trailer for office space. But that will be even better. Praise the Lord." And Velma stops in the tiny room to give Sunny another order for tapes.

I continue down to the end of the corridor to the other little room. Behind the narrow sliding door is Rhoda's office.

Rhoda Wierwille has been from the beginning — well, almost from the beginning — another pillar of the ministry. She is Dr. Wierwille's personal secretary during the week and the pianist at every Sunday night meeting. This September she celebrates her twenty-fifth year with the ministry. Her last name comes from the fact that she married Doctor's brother, Reuben, in 1963. Dressed in neatly modest apparel, her silver-gray hair wavy over her button earrings, she looks up and smiles as I slide open the door.

"Is this a good time to visit with you for a few minutes?" I ask.

"It's as good as any," she states honestly. "I'm all caught up on the mail that has to go out. It's always busy around here, but come in." She reaches across her desk to turn off the dictaphone, and continues, waving her hand in the direction of the double file cabinet.

"It certainly will be wonderful to move into the new executive office building next week. I'm just about running out of space for the new files. We're moving just in time, as far as I'm concerned."

"I wanted to hear about the early years of the ministry. I have just been talking with Uncle Harry. How is it that you came here?" I begin at the beginning.

"I guess the same way everyone got here and got together — God brought me. During the Second World War, I went to the Moody Bible Institute in Chicago to study music. I graduated in 1946, and a girlfriend and I agreed to do youth work in various churches. So we worked together for a half year until she got married. After that, I was free, so to speak, from any commitments.

"I was brought up a Mennonite from Lancaster, Pennsylvania. I always had to stand up for what I believed. At that time the Mennonites didn't believe in radio ministries because they said that Satan was the god of the air. My sister and I had appeared on a children's radio show, and when it was time to be confirmed, they held us back. My father also had become involved with a Bible College outside of the church.

"Well, the following Sunday at church, they read our names and we were all excommunicated from the church, except for our mother. But when we rose to leave, she didn't say anything. She walked out with us. You see, we all stood our ground. We knew we were doing the Lord's will and there was nothing harmful in it.

"Now I think sometimes that the Lord was preparing me for working in this ministry in my future life. You can't be swayed by what people think of you. God asks you to stand. And that's what you have to do. This ministry always takes a stand on the Word. But I know how hard it must have been for Dr. and Mrs. Wierwille because they were born and raised in the church. They were church people." Rhoda's voice fades for a few seconds.

"But anyway, in 1947, when my girlfriend got married, I was free, so I wrote to Moody to state my qualifications and make myself available for a job. Exactly the time my letter arrived there, a letter from VP came saying that he needed a musician with secretarial skills. They sent him my name. And he wrote me sending a ticket to Ohio.

"You know, I never would have come if that letter had been written on church stationery. I already was turned off by denominations. I saw how little they had to offer. But for some reason, VP wrote me that letter on Chimes Hour letterhead. I decided to come and see about the job over that Labor Day weekend and at this time the Board of Directors asked me if I would accept the job. I said yes. After this I spent a few weeks at home arranging some personal matters. I actually began working for him as minister of music and as his personal secretary in the church in Van Wert, Ohio on September 28, 1947.

"His family had moved to Van Wert in 1944, after three years in Payne, Ohio, but I don't know much about those years except what I've heard tell."

"When I came to work, they said it would be a step of faith. They could afford to pay me $18 a week. I agreed. After a couple of months, they could afford to pay me $20 a week. I had no contract, no promises when I came here. It really was a step of faith. I had to believe that money would keep coming in to pay me.

"Doctor Wierwille already had a radio program going called the Chimes Hour Youth Caravan. I arranged all the music and worked with two choirs. We had rehearsals every night of the week. During the day, I did secretarial work.

"Twenty or twenty-five young people worked on the program on a volunteer basis. They sang, played and engineered. They donated their time. We broadcasted by remote control from the church over radio station WLOK (now WIMA) Lima, Ohio a half hour, Sundays from 12:00 to 12:30 immediately following the Sunday morning service. In 1952 we worked out of Cincinnati at 4:30 to 5 Sunday afternoons, at which time we rented a private phone line and continued broadcasting direct from the church.

"The program opened with several choir songs. Seventeen minutes of music, poetry, prayer and VP teaching; then we ended with another choir song. It was a popular program. Letters came from Pennsylvania, Canada, New York, Michigan, Ohio, West Virginia, Indiana, Illinois and Kentucky. We got an average of 75 pieces of mail a day, and we had a regular mailing list of about 3000.

"VP has always had music in his heart. Look at his interest in the music groups now, "Selah" and that group from New York, "Pressed Down, Shaken Together and Running Over," and some of the others. Way Productions, the music ministry today, is an outgrowth of those early radio programs."

Rhoda pauses. I venture, "I guess there has been a great change in the type of music from choir to the folk rock the groups do today."

"Yes, lots of things are that way. It's the same Word of God we're standing on, but there's a new look about it,"

Rhoda agrees. "The growth among the young people began after Dr. Wierwille made his trip to California the winter of 1967-68. Then they began to come out here. First Steve and Sandi Heefner, then more and more others.

"Things really started speeding up after that. The young people were mostly hippies — people with long hair. They really took to the ministry because it made things fit for them."

"What did you think when they started coming here, the ones with the long hair?" I ask, curious.

"Long hair never bothered me. Our grandparents had that. But we were excited when we heard people were coming from California. Up until that time, there were mostly adults in the ministry, and the same people for years, and only a few young people. We pay no attention to how people look. To see the changes that take place in their lives — that's our reward here at Headquarters. The kids come here and work, and we love them. But we have discipline too. You can't let them run away from responsibilities. Someone has to reprove and correct them.

"I remember one young man in particular. His father was an important businessman, but you never would have known it. The first time I saw him, his clothes were dirty and torn. He was sitting in the dining room with his girlfriend. I wouldn't have given you a nickel for the two of them together. He had long hair, uncombed, a full beard and a mustache. He was barefoot, dirt just caked on his feet. The two of them felt that no one here would accept them so they had brought along their own food — seeds — and were not going to eat in the dining room.

"By the time three weeks were up, big changes had taken place. He had cleaned himself up. And by the end of the summer, you wouldn't have recognized him — he was polished and shining, took a real interest in caring for himself. He was adept in the field of woodworking, wanted to accomplish something and began working toward these goals. That's just one example. There were so many others like him.

"It's the love here that heals people. They come here; and when they hear the Word, they start growing up in giant strides. That really is our reward to see God working in a person's life before our very eyes."

"I guess things have changed a lot over the years," I remark, musing over Rhoda's observations.

"Yes, they have. Do you know that in those early years I used to keep my files in shoe boxes, so as not to spend money on cabinets? We didn't always have all of this. In 1955, I began to keep the books. We didn't even have an adding machine. We did it all manually — Uncle Harry and I.

"In the winter of 1961, we bought our first electric adding machine. It was like pennies from heaven. The piano is another example. In Van Wert, we had a Packard Grand, but we had to leave it behind in the church there. We just kept believing for $4500 for a new grand. In the meantime, I had a studio upright.

"In 1965, when the new part of the Biblical Research Center was dedicated, we met a piano technician from Covington. He wanted to sell a reconditioned grand. I could hardly believe my ears and eyes. It was completely reconditioned — new felts, new strings, everything in perfect shape for $750. It was another pennies from heaven deal because we had believed for years.

"When you come from our background, doing without for so long, and then you find things miraculously supplied by the Lord, it sure is wonderful. People today can't really comprehend it now. We did without and just kept believing.

"So you see, this is why Doctor and Uncle Harry and Velma and me, all those that have come up from way back, are very particular on how things are treated and how equipment is taken care of. We want things to last in working order as long as possible because we remember the days when we had so little."

I also find it hard to picture the old days, sitting here, knowing the life of the ministry today. I would have liked to sit here longer, to hear more stories of the old days told by Rhoda's quiet, gentle voice; but with a genuine respect for her time, I thank her for sharing the past with me, and sliding the door shut behind me, leave her to her work.

Surrounded by mental pictures from the past, I muse my way through the tiny entranceway and out of the door. The wind has risen now blowing an army of majestic clouds across the sun, which shines through them at intervals. The air chills my skin, but I believe sooner or later, spring must come, the trees will bloom. It has been a long, cold winter it seems. But even now, the snow from yesterday's sudden blizzard is completely melted and sunbeams reflect from newly-forming mud along the path. The ground has begun to thaw.

I am thinking: "Well, that's the Main Office — executives and secretaries. And yet, how different from the world where the secretaries or assistants serve the bosses. For here, according to God's Word, everyone is a servant. Everyone, no matter what his responsibilities, serves God. There is no sharp distinction here in the main offices between management and labor, or in the kitchen between the cooks and the eaters. Everyone here knows that the greatest is he who serves, and so they all serve one another, thereby serving God."

Through my musings, I suddenly see Beth Ricks, with a broad smile and a welcoming nod, walking quickly towards me across the driveway. Another Way Corps member, who took the class eight years ago at the age of 12, she greets me enthusiastically and invites me to come over and see Trailer 8, the Collating Department, where she works four hours a day. I slip my hand through her arm and we clatter across the boards together. Howard passes by us on his bicycle. His handsome angular face is full of calm determination and a quiet "Hi, girls," slips out of his mouth as he breezes by.

"You might not know it," Beth explains, "but Emogene Allen, Howard's wife is in charge of collating. You'd never know it because you don't see much of her, what with two small boys and the little baby. But she is an amazing woman. She has an office at home, out on the patio and takes care of the Bookstore. All orders for books and tapes and records go to her and she channels them to Linda in the Bookstore and Sunny in the Tape Department.

"She is also responsible for collating and mailing — that's where I work. She's very organized and efficient. She lets us be on top of it over here in Trailer 8, but she makes it clear that we can call her anytime if we have a problem. And she never bugs us, but then of course, we get our work done." Beth stops to open the door.

Trailer 8 is the same size as Trailers 6 and 7, the men's and women's trailers. We enter the patio — a large area housing the Collating and Addressing Departments. Beth goes over to her machine, pulls back the plastic cover and sits down to work.

The other half of this trailer is a cozy apartment where Pat and Nancy Johnson have been living since January. Just turned twenty, this newly-married couple was invited to come here, Pat to work on construction in his trade as a carpenter, and Nancy, willing to do whatever needed to be done. She is now in charge of collating.

The patio is a symphony of sounds, as each machine hums and stamps in its own peculiar manner. Petite Nancy, her thick dark hair falling over her shoulders, rubber thimbles on her fingers, is quickly collating the first batch of the Jonah coloring books, the same one that Tina was printing in the Print Shop earlier this morning. Neat piles of papers are stacked in rows on the long table before her. She walks up and down the row, pulling out a page at a time in order.

On the other side of the table, Angie is doing a similar operation, but at a much slower pace. (Remember, she and Paul are the ones we had breakfast with this morning.)

"You're at work already, I see," I remark to Angie.

"Yes, we went to see Howard this morning after breakfast. He got me a little room here in Trailer 8, and I'm just helping Nancy here," she says a little shyly. "I might as well work. Everyone else is working. There's no one to talk to," she adds with a shrug. And then after a pause, "Paul and I are definitely staying for the class. Paul has moved into a house in town, and he's working somewhere too this morning."

I turn to Nancy to ask about the flow of her work.

"The work comes in spurts," she tells me. "Last week we didn't have much work. Just little collating jobs came up suddenly which had to be done immediately. When there's a lot, Linda or some of the other girls come and help me. So we have to be here all the time, but last week when we didn't have much work, we shampooed the rugs here and washed all the windows. We had a good time."

Behind Nancy, Tim, the same Tim we had breakfast with this morning, is working the small offset press. As he works, he sings: "O Sole Mio" in exaggerated falsetto, interjecting dramatic operatic gestures. I pick up one of his freshly printed sheets.

"I'm running off piano music to go with the song books — one musical score goes out with every order of song books — blue books for the adults and orange for the children," he sings to me to the titters of all the others in the room. I give him a round of applause and he bows elegantly. "If you think Act I is good, wait till you see Act III!" he exclaims, over the thumping of the little press.

Beth is by now deep into her work at the manual addressing machine, a table arrangement where she is stamping out a new card file. I watch over her shoulder the speedy movement of her fingers.

"The thing that takes the longest is changes of address. People just keep moving. That takes about a third of the time at this machine. The whole mailing list is over 4000, and the magazine subscription is about 2500. I've gotten so that I can do it in one morning. The whole mailing list takes about six hours now." Beth talks to me in spurts as she works, not taking her eyes off the little metal plates in front of her.

Cathi Yeremian is handling the automatic addressing machine, stamping addresses on the latest issue of The Way magazine. Beside her there stands an automatic folding machine, on the other side, an automatic stapler and farther down a trimming machine.

Beth calls me back and stops working for a minute.

"Do you know, I just remembered that Emogene Allen used to do all these things by herself, with some volunteer help now and then, until last fall when Cathi and I and then Nancy came in. We've never been so busy as now — so many more people, so many more classes to use the materials.

"There are machines that do these jobs in one operation, but they cost a lot more and then we wouldn't have anything to do. It's right for now. We have time between operations to do all the work so that it's in good shape. This summer, collating will move to the Outreach House in town along with printing and mailing, and then things will change. But God will provide," she adds and turns back to the stamping.

They have a lot of work to do. But I have seen the entire procedure. "Thanks for the visit," I say over the clacking of work. "Thank you, Beth, for inviting me to see. Have a fabulous morning and I'll see you all at lunch," I conclude, and a shower of good-byes follows me out of the door.

I walk along the wooden boards back out to the driveway in time to see two unfamiliar people standing beside an unfamiliar car. It is not unusual to see strangers suddenly appear here, for nearly every day people stop by: ambassadors to be reassigned, believers from all over the country or from local areas, visitors and guests just curious to take a look at what is happening here — like Angie and Paul who arrived late last night — or parents and relatives of people living here who come to get a closer look at what they're up to.

Then I recall the announcement yesterday — the roving ambassadors are coming in for a stopover. Introducing myself, I ask them if that's who they are.

"I'm Steve Aldridge," the heavy-set, clean-cut young man replies, "and this is Marcia Faulk; we're the 'Ambassadors on Wheels'."

"I thought that might be who you are. I've heard a lot about you, during announcements and prayers. It's great you're home. What is it that you do when you're on the road?" I ask them.

Steve laughs meaningfully, "Everything. You name it. You know there are over a hundred ambassadors in the field. Well, we travel from one group to another, wherever we're needed. Our home is wherever we are. We serve them however and whenever we can. We might help them find jobs and find a place to stay. We exhort, comfort and also spread the good news of whatever's happening in other parts of the country. It's a great job.

"People out on the field can get to feeling in a rut, like they're all alone, and that's where we come in. We call Craig every week. He's in charge of all the ambassadors, and we ask him where we should go next — and he tells us to move on or stay. And we do it."

"We're sure learning a lot," Marcia contributes with a toss of her short yellow hair. "We just pulled in and we're on our way to the Wierwille house basement to see Reverend Cummins and Craig."

"I'll walk over with you," I suggest, wanting to hear more about their life on wheels. We walk slowly down the paved driveway.

"Well, where have you been lately?" I ask, wanting to get a clearer picture.

"We started on a pilot trip on January 9th in Orlando, Florida. We're both from East Carolina University and we heard we were on. So we drove back there, packed up our stuff and rolled in here to get our instructions," Steve recounts. "After that, our first stop was Bowling Green where we sat in on the branch meeting — Kathy Rolsten is the branch leader there. Then it was Flint, Michigan, for two days, Lansing, Belding and then Philadelphia, Pennsylvania. There were some opportunities there, which we worked with. From there it was Washington, D. C., then Long Island and Boston. After that, we got to Rochester and Geneva, New York and Cleveland and Akron, Ohio, and here we are."

I am interested to hear more. "That's a lot of miles. But what do you do? How do you just come into an area where people don't know you and work with them? It must be hard."

"It sure is a chance to walk in wisdom," Steve agrees with a laugh, suggesting understatement. "I guess it boils down to reminding the people of things they forgot to do. They watch us. And we have to watch ourselves, and be our best at all times. We make suggestions, but we do the most when we set excellent examples. We have to know the Word and be on top of it spiritually. You can't be heavy or people turn off. But you have to make your point."

"But how do you work with the people?" I insist.

"We start by having individual raps with the people and then we meet with them all together. We build them up in any way we can. And we never see the results of what we have done. We just believe God big.

"Here's an example. In one particular area there were three ambassadors together. They eat together, meet together, witness together, do everything but sleep together. It's like a marriage almost, and sometimes personalities get in the way. We're all working toward being more spiritual, but it's easy sometimes to start looking at the flesh. That's probably the biggest opportunity. It boils down to knowing who the leader is and hanging in with him no matter what.

"Each group of ambassadors has one coordinator. In this particular area, the coordinator was a guy and there were two girls working with him. One of the girls had been involved in the ministry longer than he. She felt she had more knowledge so she was exalting herself above the other two instead of working together. She didn't respect the coordinator.

"Maybe sense-knowledgewise she did have more knowledge, but spiritually she could have believed God big and worked with the others to get the Word out. That's our goal, to get past the personality differences in the flesh and get that Word out.

"Well, we sat down and rapped with her and after a while she began to get honest with herself. Something we've really learned is when we talk to people individually we just talk about that person, get them open. We let our hair down, take our shoes off and let it all hang out. That way trust develops quickly. There's no profit in talking to one person about the others because then fear creeps in that you'll talk to the others about him. That way everyone gets suspicious and nothing gets done.

"So we talk to each one about himself, what's on his heart." Then we meet with them all together and get everything ironed out. I'm sure learning a lot every day." Steve finishes as we come to the Wierwille home.

"Where do you go next?" I ask them. "You cover the country."

"Yes, that's another thing we thank God for every day — how we never get lost on the roads in all these unfamiliar places. But where we go next, I don't know. Craig might tell us right now, and we'll be out of here tonight, or tomorrow. It doesn't matter. We're ready to go wherever we're needed. But it sure is great to spend a couple of days here at Headquarters, or even fifteen minutes. Everybody loves you so much here; you can just relax and dig it. It's really restful." Steve pauses at the door.

"It's fantastic to hear it from you firsthand," I tell him. "I'll go in with you. I had something I wanted to ask Reverend Cummins about anyway." Steve holds the door for us, and in a row we troop down the narrow staircase to the basement.

The Wierwille home is a remodeled old Ohio farmhouse. Tastefully furnished and roomy, the two main floors are occupied by Dr. Wierwille, his wife Dorothea, and their two youngest children, John Paul and Sara, who boarded the school bus earlier this morning. Doctor's office is on the main floor, in a room added to the original structure several years ago.

This also is part of the order here on the farm. With nearly fifty people in residence, several together in family groups, achieving that delicate balance between privacy and fellowship could be an area of friction. However, it is not. Each family, each individual has the space he needs for privacy and no more. Furthermore, there is other space available for fellowship — getting together to work or play, inside or outside in pleasant surroundings.

Take the Wierwille home, for example. The two main floors are reserved for the family and their private life, but the basement is utilized for other people as needed. The entire house is not kept in shrouded seclusion. It is not off-limits to people. On the contrary, there is a constant flow of people in and out of certain parts of it. And yet the other part is private. Discipline is a part of love, and here love is manifested by a general respect for other people's space, an awareness and genuine caring for other people's needs.

Could you for a moment imagine eleven people working daily in the family room in your basement without intruding in your life? It sounds like people trooping through the house, milling around, loud laughter, clutter, unemptied ash-trays, overflowing wastebaskets, annoyance and hassle.

It could be that way. But as I said in the beginning, this place is out of this world. And it is. One of those things you suddenly become vividly aware of here is that part of the Christian walk where people bear their own burdens, take care of themselves, their own space, and at the same time are constantly aware and considerate of others.

But back to the Wierwille basement. Eleven people have their desk space here. The side door that Steve held for us is right at the top of a narrow staircase leading there. Thus people coming and going with a minimum of noise, hardly disturb the events or running of the main house.

Coming down the stairs we enter a furnished kitchen, left over from the days when the basement housed other people on the farm before the mobile homes were brought in. Now it is used for occasional receptions and parties held down here, thereby avoiding intrusion in the house kitchen upstairs.

To the left of the basement kitchen, a long room called the fireplace room — cozy yet spacious — is used for meet-ings, parties or overnight lodging. Mementos of hunting and fishing trips decorate the walls. But for the perking coffee machine with its glowing red eye, the room is empty of people.

Straight ahead from the kitchen is an even larger long room referred to as the Wierwille basement, where all those people I mentioned before work daily and sometimes late into the night. It is a good-sized room, but the green billiard table in its center limits the space. Desks line the walls, but at intervals, and such a peacefulness pervades the room that you might suppose at first glance that only two or three people work here. An atmosphere of diligence breathes in the room.

A wave of greetings and embraces meet Steve and Marcia. After a short exchange with everyone, the two settle down with Craig, the coordinator of all the ambassadors.

Near the doorway, Doug Murphy, head of the planning committee for the Rock of Ages, surveys a large ground plan of the Sidney Fairgrounds where the festival of teaching and music might be held to accommodate this year's crowd.

At another desk, Earl, blond ex-college football hero from North Carolina, goes through a card file. Branch leader of the Miami Valley, he is currently spiritually responsible for over 600 graduates of the 'Power for Abundant Living' Class spread out in 15 counties in this area of Ohio.

There is Dave Craley, 28, ex-advertising and public relations executive from San Francisco, now doing public relations for The Way.

At another desk, Patte Adams works as Craig's secretary, her Way Corps job. Naomi Bliss, another Way Corps member, earphones on her head, is listening to a tape in the long process of preparing a detailed catalog of the tape library.

Bo Reahard, who researches Orientalisms in the Bible, has his desk here. Also Mike Smith, the curly-haired producer of Way Productions from Wichita, Kansas. Both their desks are unoccupied just now, the empty chairs drawn neatly in out of the way.

Nancy Bowen has her desk here when she works with Earl. And Leonard Ochs works here. An ex-army officer with two growing children, ages 13 and 10, he handles legal administrative matters, particularly estate planning.

As I make my way into the room, Leonard addresses me.

"I bet you'd be interested in the report Dave Anderson and I have just completed on the ministry. Doctor Wierwille asked us to make a survey of all the programs of the ministry to break down the man-hours, expenses and materials, so that we can check out the allocation of resources. We want to know exactly what's happening."

"I have heard nothing about it," I perk up my ears. "But it sounds interesting. What have you come up with?"

"Do you know how many separate programs we carry in this ministry?" he challenges me.

"I really can't guess," I come back after a moment's consideration. After all, it's a family enterprise. Everyone works hard. If they boasted or complained I might have more of an idea. But everyone does his work, and when people talk they say something edifying like: "God bless you."

"I don't know, Leonard. How many?"

"There are 38 separate programs all over the country. The 'Power for Abundant Living' Class is just one of them. With this breakdown of factors involved we will be better able to utilize our people, time and money. We're striving to be organized in the best possible manner as we grow. With the campaign coming up and new people coming in, we need to be even more efficient to be effective. It's not something haphazard you leave to chance," he concludes.

I suddenly recall something Dr. Wierwille taught one time, how believers in the Word of God live as though Jesus Christ were coming back any minute — full of hope, enthusiasm and expectation, and at the same time, work as though it were years away. No one knows the day, but God. Therefore a Christian working with the knowledge and wisdom God has made available through His Word, until that day plans, organizes, works out minute details perfectly to get the daily results God has promised us.

"Thanks for letting me know about the report," I tell Leonard. "I wouldn't have thought there were 38. You're working with Doug, too, on the Rock of Ages this year?" I ask, having heard that recently.

"That's right. It's five months away, but there's a lot to be done even now. For instance, we're having a dinner here for all the mayors and officials of the surrounding towns in May to inform them about our plans for the Rock of Ages. Last year rumors spread that there would be drugs, drunks, violence — I don't know what else. Not knowing us, many people expected trouble. The police force was mustered, on the ready. Of course, nothing like that happened. They thought it would be another confusion like Woodstock. So this year we're inviting them all here to let them know what to expect, so they can relax; lots of people high on the Word of God, not drugs."

"Sounds like excellent public relations," I propose, "to stop the rumors at the top. I remember last year — police cars cruising and private citizens armed. They sure had a lot of fear. They didn't quite know how to take it when nothing happened. Well, I want to speak with Reverend Cummins while I'm here. I'll see you later, Leonard."

Now I'm really glad to be here. I hadn't planned to come here today. And yet, a particular question had been on my mind for the last few days that I simply could not let go. I know now for certain that it's Reverend Walter Cummins I had wanted to ask.

At 25, Reverend Cummins is Dr. Wierwille's assistant. Walter has a youthful face and neatly trimmed light brown hair, bespeaking his background as a normal midwestern young man. His manner is gentle, his speech soft-spoken and unhurried, speckled with a simple country kind of humor, reminding me of a Lincoln in his youth — plain, in the American grain, and, at the same time, intensely human.

It is Reverend Cummins who takes over some of Dr. Wierwille's responsibilities when the Doctor is ministering in other parts of the country. It is he who speaks the Word of God with simple boldness from a wealth of personal research and a thorough knowledge of Greek. He also coordinates all research projects assigning them to Corps members and others on the research staff. For all his responsibilities, he is always approachable, as are all the people here, including those I have called the "executives" and Dr. Wierwille.

I approach Walter's desk near the door to ask if he has a little time to talk with me now.

"Sure, I have time, sit down," he invites me gesturing to a chair near his desk. "Did you come to see what we do here? Well, the real exciting time is when we have our pool game right after lunch," he continues with a smile. "That's when things really cook around here."

"If I'd known, I would have come after lunch," I toss out. "But right now I have a question on the book of Acts. You know where Paul and Barnabas have a fight? I don't remember exactly where it is, but I was reading it the other day, and I thought: 'How come two great men of God had such a sharp contention that they split up? Why should God tell us about that? What's the profit to know about that argument?'

From the shelf of books behind him Walter pulls out a Bible and flips the pages.

"Are you referring to this part, here at the end of Acts 15?" he asks, turning his Bible so I can read it right-side-up.

"That's it. Here, beginning in verse 36: 'And some days after Paul said unto Barnabas, Let us go again and visit our brethren in every city where we have preached the word of the Lord, *and see* how they do. And Barnabas determined to take with them John, whose surname was Mark. But Paul thought not good to take him with them, who departed from them from Pamphylia, and went not with them to the work. And the contention was so sharp between them, that they departed asunder one from another: and so Barnabas took Mark, and sailed unto Cyprus; And Paul chose Silas, and departed ....' Do you see what I mean? Paul and Barnabas had been working together up till then, preaching, doing miracles. God was with both of them. How could they have such a falling out? And what can we today learn from that?" I pause, scrutinizing Walter's face.

"Back here in chapter 13, you see, John Mark had been with them in Pamphylia — and then, instead of sticking with them he had tripped out. See here in verse 13, 'And John departing from them returned to Jerusalem.' We don't know any details. We just know what the Word tells us — John Mark must have tripped out.

"Now here in chapter 15, the Apostle Paul was the leader. The leader gets the revelation from God, how to lead. Sometimes it may look strange what the leader says, strange to your senses mind. Maybe it looked to Barnabas like John Mark should have another chance, after he blew it in Pamphylia. That's speculation. But the results show it.

"You see, after Barnabas leaves Paul, he is never mentioned again in the book of Acts or anywhere. The book of Acts is the record of the growth and movement of the first century Church. It follows the acts of the apostles. After the contention got sharp between them and Barnabas left, there was nothing more to record about him.

"The rest of the book of Acts sticks with Paul. He was with God. The result was: 'so mightily grew the Word of God and prevailed,' through Paul's ministry." Walter pauses. "Does that help you?"

I am thoughtful. "But what can we learn from that today in our walk? It still amazes me how two great men of God, after going through so much together, could fall out like that, with the growth of the Church and all that was happening."

"I guess we're all human," Walter remarks with a smile. "Everything is in God's foreknowledge. He knows if someone is going to stand a week, a month or ten years or a lifetime. Barnabas did a great work when he was on the Word. There was profit for God in his stand. Now, he had free will, like we all do, to go his own way or God's."

"But he thought he was right in taking John Mark. And Paul thought he was right in not taking John Mark. Each one must have thought that he was doing God's will. How do we know today what the will of God is?" I ask.

"That's right. They both thought they were right, had their good reasons, but you see, from all indications in the Word, Paul the apostle was the spiritual leader. He was responsible to God. And anyone else goes with the spiritual leader. That's why we go with the leader, believing God he's receiving the necessary guidance from God. That's the like-mindedness the Word exhorts us all to achieve together."

"But isn't that like-mindedness kind of like a herd of sheep following blindly?"

"Like-mindedness is not the same as conformity," Walter corrects my view. "Like-mindedness is knowing and believing the Word of God together to the end that you all walk out on it together. In the Word, there are set forth gift ministries — apostles, evangelists, pastors, teachers and prophets. Paul had the gift ministry of an apostle and was the spiritual leader at that time. Now God set forth these gift ministries for the perfection of the Body of Christ. Since they are there, they must be needed.

"Paul grew into being the greatest leader of the first century Church. He was the only one able to receive the fullness of the revelation of the mystery that was hid for ages — the mystery of the Church as the Body of Christ, and Christ in us, the hope of glory. Like-mindedness on the part of Barnabas would have informed him to follow Paul.

"We come up against these situations all the time in our ministry. It's the Body of Christ working together. The members of the Body must be like-minded. Take three ambassadors today out in the field. One of them is the coordinator, the leader. God gives him the guidance. The others believe God is giving him the guidance and stick with him. If he says, 'Let's go witnessing today,' and one of the others says, 'I've got to do the laundry,' and the other says, 'It's going to rain,' then they end up just arguing with each other or sulking and not getting the Word out. But if they fall in with him, all go witnessing, and it turns out pouring cats and dogs, the leader will learn to check out the spiritual weather report or something. Furthermore, that bond of love is built up between them. Love is what keeps the Body of Christ together."

"I'm beginning to see it now." I say to Walter, relieved. It's great to have questions answered. It's great that the Word doesn't condemn. I'm glad Paul never said to Barnabas: 'I told you so. You were wrong, you idiot.' Barnabas is just never mentioned again. But Paul's example is there for us to learn from and follow — someone who kept on doing the Word of God even when people around him tripped out. And Paul kept getting the results God promises: "So mightily grew the Word of God and prevailed."

"That's great. Thank you. I see it now," I reiterate. Walter leans back in his chair. Relaxed and smiling warmly, his whole being expresses strength and meekness. I suddenly realize that I know very little about him, in spite of the number of times I have thrilled to his teaching. The room is quiet and he seems to have all the time in the world right now. My curiosity is whetted and I take the initiative.

"When did you become involved in this ministry? How did you hear about it?" I ask him.

"My mother took the 'Power for Abundant Living' Class here in the fall of 1961. It was the second Foundational Class here at the farm after Dr. Wierwille and his family moved here. You see, we lived in New Bremen, the next town over. She kept telling me how good everything was, and I kept saying, 'Yes, yes, I'd like to go but I have too much homework.' That went on for a few weeks and finally, one day my mother said, 'All right, don't come then.'

"So I went. The class was taught right here in this very basement room because the Biblical Research Center had not been built. The first night I learned more than I had ever learned in church all my life. I was 15 then, a sophomore in high school.

"The basement was pretty full — seventy-five to a hundred people. I got very excited and decided to take the class. I just jumped in, thought it was the greatest thing in the world. Danny Shroyer and I used to come together — he is in the Mailing and Receiving Department here now.

"The following summer I got a job in New Bremen and paid all my own expenses for Summer School and camp. I worked all day, but I was here every evening.

"My junior year in high school, I decided to sit around and just research the Word. My grades went down, and at the end of the year Dr. Wierwille talked to me and said I should go to college. I was kind of hurt at first. I wanted to get right into the ministry full-time. I guess it's like the record of Paul and Barnabas. The leader does the leading. When Dr. Wierwille said that to me, I thought at first he was all wrong; but now, I see that his guidance was the best because I have much more to offer the ministry. I had time to grow up and learn. When I was ready, the ministry was ready for me. Everything worked out just right.

"That junior year is when I opened up a Greek book and started studying on my own. I didn't learn a whole lot though — not the depth of it. I guess it was a case of lots of zeal and not too much knowledge of how to go about things.

"December of 1961 was when the original part of the Bible Center was completed. The basement got too small fast. In 1963, my mother and Uncle Harry were married there, the same summer that Rhoda and Reuben Wierwille got married. That was a summer of weddings. The addition on the Bible Center was ready for use in January, 1965. The ministry was really growing.

"Most of the people in those days were local — from Columbus, Indiana and the Toledo area. We had a great vision then of the Word reaching out over Ohio. We were all pretty straight — no long hairs — more adults than young people.

"After high school, I went to Asbury College in Kentucky — that's where I started a serious study of Greek. My major was math, my minor journalism and my great hobby was Greek.

"But I had a few opportunities at Asbury," Walter chuckles to himself, his eyes sparkling. "You see, I was asked to leave there because I spoke in tongues and was teaching it to others in the dorm from the Word of God. By January, I had a twig fellowship going in the dorm, and in March the Dean of Men called me in.

"He said he heard that I spoke in tongues and that I didn't go to church. (Asbury has religious affiliations, you see.) He told me to quit teaching or they'd ask me to leave. I said I'd pray about it. That night I called Dr. Wierwille and told him what had happened. He said it was more important to finish my education.

"When I hung up the phone, I was kind of disappointed. But just then, Dr. Wierwille called me back to say, 'I just got quiet with the Father and He says it's time to make a stand. Go ahead. If they throw you out, sit outside the classroom, and we'll come down with some people to sit with you.'

"That really encouraged me. We just continued to meet for the next two months. Nobody bothered us. And then I got a letter from the administration informing me that I was not expected to come back again that fall.

"It was a mutual parting of ways. I transferred to Ohio State and got married that summer — to Joyce Stork, Velma's daughter."

"You mean Velma in the office? I never realized that your wife was Velma's daughter. And your mother married Uncle Harry. That puts you right in the family," I interject.

"We're all in the family really," Walter corrects. "It sure is something how God works in our lives for the very best, even before we are aware of it. Sometimes years before. You never know how it's going to work out. That's God's business. You just believe God and know it's going to be the very best.

"I started teaching Greek here in Summer School in 1966, 1967 and again in 1969. I figured as a teacher in the local schools, I'd be able to support myself and have the summers free to study and teach here. So that's how it happened for a while. Then I was invited to come here full-time. Looking back now, I can see how everything fell into place just right. The best." Walter comes to a stop in his narrative.

"What is it particularly that you are researching now?" I ask him.

"I work with the Corps a lot. We have several projects going. We're studying the last week of the life of Jesus, for example, putting together all the accounts from the Gospels. Then several people are doing a study on the use of colors in the Word. That's pretty exciting. We will have something written up on it soon.

"You see, if it's God's Word, everything has to fit together perfectly, every word, every use of color, every incident has a purpose. That's the premise we start with. Then we work from there." The conversation winds itself to a halt.

"It sure has been interesting talking with you," I conclude, rising and pushing my chair back into place.

"If you have another question, we're here," Walter adds, encouraging me. And everything has been uttered.

I make my way back through the basement kitchen and up the narrow staircase. At the top of the steps, I pause, taking in the sounds of the main house. Everything is silent, but for the ticking of a clock. I guess everyone is out and, turning about, I step out of the door we entered a short time before. A long concrete veranda parallels the house along this wall.

It is still cold this morning in March. Behind the house, the lawns, grass cropped from last fall, in subtle shades of yellow and brown, are withered under the chill of passing winter. Dark evergreens populate the grounds here and there. A ways beyond, a white trellis is covered by naked, twining vines.

The clouds by now have overwhelmed the sun, captured the sky. Under its overcast light, the pond, ice all but melted, calm and gray, reflects the diffused grayness of the sky. Beyond the trellis, a rough log bridge reaches over the little stream called the River Jordan. Harmless now, it will swell and swirl with the spring rains soon, I suppose. Half a mile away, across the flat expanse of fields, on the main road, Route 29, cars cruise by, now from the right, now from the left, looking like tiny toys in the distance.

The serenity of the grounds engulfs me momentarily. I believe I shall carry this stillness with me anywhere I go. "He leads me beside the still waters." God's peace is everywhere, and I rest and refresh myself in it.

Oh yes, I had thought to take a look at the new executive office building today, to see the progress. Inhaling deeply the peace that surrounds me, I start across the driveway to the new building.

In front of the garage, a motley collection of vehicles are parked. I see tall, blond Dave Buschmann, the W.O.W. ambassador, dodging to and fro around the shop. I have not seen him since the early morning meeting. Seems like a year. He is on the job, repairing cars, motors, machinery. Someone else's head suddenly emerges from under the hood of a car. I recognize Barry Jones, a Way Corps member, who works with Dave in the shop. The two young men exchange a few words, which I cannot discern from this distance. There is the resounding clatter of tools on steel and both of them disappear from my view.

One vehicle in particular catches my attention. White and new, stands the motorcoach that came in yesterday afternoon. Now I recall, something about packing it up today. Doctor said he'd be packing it today, getting ready for the Advanced Class in Rye. The door swings open. Someone must be inside.

A series of quick steps approach me from behind, and in a minute Nancy Bowen is addressing me.

"Are you going to the new office building?" I respond with a nod. "I'll walk over with you. I have to talk to Susan. She is going to help me make my wedding dress."

Nancy and I fall into step. Nancy is slender, delicately-built and has long, dark hair falling alongside a freckled, heart-shaped face, dramatically accented by her large blue eyes. She was the hostess in the dining room at breakfast.

"What do you do besides hostess and work with Earl?" I take the opportunity to ask her.

"Well, things have changed since last week," Nancy begins. "Hostesses rotate. We all need experience in this field, all the Way Corps women. So we change off. This is my week.

"But as for working with Earl, that has been changed. We've been engaged since last summer, you know, and I started helping him with his work this fall when he became branch leader for this area of Ohio. I started by doing some of his typing, and then other things that had to be done, and we became more and more like business partners. We'd have supper together in the evening, and we would still be clicking on the work.

"The principle involved here is that I was trying to help him do the work, rather than helping him be able to do the work." Nancy emphasizes the end of her sentence. "I'm just beginning to see it now, what was really happening. We were having a lot of pressure on the job, so Earl talked to Dr. Wierwille and he changed my job. Now I work in the Printing Department. Doctor was so loving about it. He understood what was happening. He said I should be Earl's sweetie and not his business partner. That was last week, and since then everything has gotten much smoother between us."

"When are you getting married?" I ask her.

"We're both in the second year of the Corps. We will graduate in August and then get married here on the farm, a small wedding. Then we'll be ready to be sent out wherever we are needed to minister the Word," Nancy relates simply.

The new office building smells of newness — fresh paint, clean wood, recently-poured concrete. A two-story structure, it is rectangular in shape, covered with brown wooden boards. The ground floor is still under serious construction. Full of building materials — cans of paint, boards, machinery, tools and sacks of cement — it is, however, already divided into two large sections.

One part will contain a shop and a workroom, including laundry facilities for residents. The other end will contain restroom facilities — rows of showers, sinks and toilets — for people camping or just on the grounds for the day. Pat Johnson, the brown-bearded carpenter from Trailer 8, is hammering together storage shelves, while Mr. Owens, Mr. Randall, and Mr. Ulrey, all working in construction, hold a short conference in one corner.

The entrances to the upstairs offices are separate. We walk up the unpainted wooden steps, our footsteps echoing in the newness of the building. It is quiet and empty, but for the gentle taps of a hammer on carpet tacks.

Bo and Sky are laying wall-to-wall carpet here. They work, crouching barefoot on the fuzzy rug. Along both walls, doors open into eight separate offices. There is one conference room the size of two offices together; and stretching through the middle of the building is a large open area for the secretarial pool. The space is simply and efficiently designed. In each office and at each end of the buildings, large windows look over the flat fields, over all the other buildings on the farm. The effect is almost like being in a skyscraper. The windows are already spotlessly clean, and the area is bright and airy, light and refreshing.

In the conference room, Susan has been sewing draperies for all the windows. Large piles of folded fabric line the walls — plaids, prints, solid colors. At one end of the room the small light from her sewing machine glares against the wall. In the middle, a full-sized plywood board on legs is her makeshift worktable.

Nancy pulls a pattern out of her pocket and hands it to Susan. They begin discussing variations, Susan proposing alternatives in her sweet Southern drawl.

I leave them to work out Nancy's wedding gown together and I make a final tour of the offices. Each room has two walls of paneling and two of wall paper. Every office is decorated differently. The old office trailer runs through my mind. It sure will be a welcome change when everyone moves in here next week. 'Just in time,' Velma said. You don't get it until you need it. And when you need it, that's when you get it because God is always on time. No need to fret or worry with God.

Then the old office trailer will become a tape listening area and a study area. That's just in time too, for the influx of numbers of Summer School students and the new Corps members coming in June. It all works out for the best, like Walter said a few minutes ago.

I start down the fragrantly clean steps. "It's a good time to take a look at the new motorcoach," runs through my mind. I have not had a chance to survey the inside since it arrived yesterday. Emerging from the new building, I see even from this distance that the motorcoach has been reparked. Beside it, stands the smaller old camper-truck that had been the mainstay of Doctor's long distance transportation until now. Side by side, both vehicles' doors are opened and there is evidence of movement from the old to the new. At the front wheel of the motorcoach little Koko , Mrs. Wierwille's miniature white poodle, licks his paws calmly.

Dr. Wierwille is packing the new motorcoach. Howard's bicycle is parked beside it. On the steps, he and Howard survey the space within, laying out exactly what goes where and how. Then they walk through, opening and measuring each cabinet.

"I want all the hunting and fishing gear here," Doctor is saying, indicating one of the compartments in a bench. "And the tape recorder and radio up here," he points to an overhead cabinet, then swings it open. "But we'll have to saw that shelf out to get it in."

One way to see what's happening is to help, so I ask if there's anything I can do.

Dr. Wierwille regards me warmly. His face is rugged and ruddy. Energy flows from his smile. His eyes sharp and blue as steel are set off by a fan of smile-wrinkles at each temple. His expression is open, exposed, yet completely unafraid and in no way defensive. His hair, thick, brown-to-graying is partly covered by a charcoal felt hat. Even in his worn denims and light blue workshirt today, his appearance is striking, with his tall stature and athletic carriage.

"Well, bless your heart, honey," he speaks slowly, kindly. "You can vacuum the cabinets before we pack them," Doctor accepts my offer, indicating a small vacuum cleaner on the rug.

"When are you going to fill the water tank?" he turns again to Howard. "I want it done soon. If there are any leaks or weak spots, now's the time to find out. I want everything checked out before I get on the road. (A pause) How's the generator working?"

I set to work vacuuming every compartment thoroughly. The roar of the little motor fills the room. Once finished, I join Mrs. Wierwille in the old van. She is emptying all the drawers of the kitchen. All the implements are carried to the house to be washed, dried and checked over. She polishes the silver, counting out a complete set for six, and then sets every piece neatly back into the washed silverware tray.

Unostentatious in appearance, Mrs. Wierwille, or Dotsie as she is affectionately called, has a gentle manner which manifests warmth and wisdom. Not one to compete for the spotlight, she stays unnoticed in the background on many occasions when her husband is teaching; and yet in her husband's absence she promptly steps into many of his responsibilities with boldness and confidence. She shows a quiet strength of character, yet without competitiveness. She speaks up when something needs to be said and at other times is not particularly talkative. Although not large in height or build, she stands straight and dignified. Her dark hair, streaked with gray, always looks well cared for and she dresses informally with good taste.

"Where would you like this, Vic?" she addresses her husband respectfully, holding up an olive-colored padded jumpsuit for cold weather activities.

"All the hunting gear can go in that seat compartment, I guess," he answers, slipping loaded cartridges into the belt of a light-weight hunting jacket. "Where are the boots? They can go in on the bottom," he adds.

Mike Smith, just inside the garage is saddlesoaping the boots and cleaning all the hunting rifles. Surrounded by these accessories, he grins as he works, now and then pushing a stray lock of hair out of his eyes.

Nothing looks brand new. Everything shows signs of use, but all is in perfect working order. Doctor looks over each piece of clothing, checking pockets, looking for evidences of dirt, holes, missing buttons or broken zippers that might impede it's usefulness at a moment's notice. Everything is cleaned, repaired, scrutinized, folded and carefully stored. Everything has its place in this space.

Mrs. Wierwille shows him what she is putting into the new motorcoach drawers. He watches the operation, studiously aware of every rubberband, paper clip, toothpick, bandaid, tube of glue. There is everything needed for any eventuality and not one extraneous item. He takes it all in, to know where to put his hands on what he needs when he needs it. A meticulous thoroughness is certainly one of Doctor's qualities. Whether in packing a trailer or in researching the Word or in teaching the Corps how to make a more effective presentation, Dr. Wierwille gives himself to it with systematic thoroughness.

Howard has gone and returned with a handsaw to eliminate the obstructing shelf. Mrs. Wierwille is bringing in the freshly washed pots and skillet for the new kitchen. Setting them down, she first lines all the cabinet shelves with self-sticking paper. Everyone works together calmly. Not many words are exchanged, only the necessary ones.

"It'll take me another day or two to pack this thing up right," Doctor is saying. "And then it will take a few weeks for me to find anything," and he gives us his hearty belly laugh. "That's why we have to pack up now, three weeks before the Advanced Class, so that by the time we get there, I'll know where to find everything."

The motorcoach is comfortably furnished. I see that Doctor shapes this space also, as he does the entire farm, and the house. He creates peace and order around him to make it work for him, to fill his needs. The space that surrounds him reflects his own inner peace and order. Yes, everything in here will be in perfect readiness by the time he leaves, and he will take a little piece of this farm with him to Rye so he can rest no matter what else is happening around him.

The public address system cracks the air: "Dr. Wierwille, Dr. Wierwille, there is a long distance phone call for you on 2522," and then repeats. Without hesitating, Doctor turns and strides across the driveway into the house.

Outside the garage, I notice Paul sweeping out the inside of the gold station wagon.

"I see you're working already," I call out to him from the motorcoach window. He looks up and around not seeing at first glance where my voice is coming from. I wave and his eyes find me.

"Yeh, we went to see Howard Allen this morning after breakfast; we're staying for the class," he calls back smiling.

"That's what Angie just told me over in Trailer 8. That's great. You'll love every minute of it," I assure him.

"Yeh, there's something about this place. Don't know what it is yet," Paul's voice fades and he sets to sweeping out the other side of the car.

The minutes pass unnoticed and then with a rush of air, Doctor is back in the motorcoach.

"That was Peter Wade calling from Australia. We talk every week or two. He says they're having a class now. A tape class. Sends his love to all the saints," and then turning directly to me as if to anticipate a question, he continues. "Peter Wade came here for the first time in 1965. He saw an ad for the Holy Spirit book in a Christian magazine. Later he came here again with his family. They stayed for three years. He had a lot to do with the magazine — what J. Fred does now in the Print Shop, he used to do. And teach. You can hear him on tape. I guess he did a lot of other things around here too. Now he has several twigs going in Australia. We sent four W.O.W. ambassadors over there to get things moving.

"I bet the radio will fit right in there now," Doctor remarks, addressing Howard, who slips the radio into the space.

Through the air, the loud speaker clicks on again: "Ten minutes till lunch now. Ten minutes till lunch. Will somebody please ring the bell." Only a few seconds pass and a clanging of the old iron dinner bell resounds over the grounds. The hunting hounds in their kennels add a chorus of mournful yaps and howls. The sounds die down.

In the motorcoach, everyone unhurriedly finishes up whatever he is doing. One by one, people from all corners of the farm, from all types of work, trickle in the direction of the basement of the Biblical Research Center. Mrs. Wierwille makes a last trip into the house. Doctor and Howard discuss a final detail, and I walk down the paved driveway in the direction of the food, to satisfy the rumblings of my stomach.

People come by ones or twos, occasionally a threesome. You would never guess how many people live and work here.

"Hi, did you have a wonderful morning?" one person addresses someone else.

"It was terrific. Bless you," comes the response. The darkening noonday sky and the blustering of the March wind do not cool the warmth and light of the spirit.

# Afternoon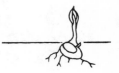

*Afternoon*

*T*he basement of the Biblical Research Center has a festive atmosphere at lunchtime. Delightful scents of hot, fresh food fill my nostrils, as I make my way to the tables. Six tables are set up now, which means 60 people, for at lunchtime staff members who are here for the day share in the meal.

In the next five minutes the dining room fills with people and greetings, everyone enjoying this hour of rest from work and sweet fellowship over food. I don't know what I have been doing all morning, but I am famished and silently rejoicing that the platters of hot food are already set out.

Lunch is actually called "dinner" — the big meal for the day — whereas supper is on the light side. Today we have oval platters piled high with crusty brown fried chicken, baby lima beans, a bowl heaped with millet, and a green salad. There is always something raw at every meal, and also some kind of seeds. Today we have sesame seeds, but other days it might be flax seeds or shelled sunflower seeds. Everyone uses the seeds differently. Some people sprinkle them on salad, on millet, or on the vegetables, and others have a mound of seeds mixed with honey as a sort of handmade dessert.

"Please find your seats," Nancy, this week's hostess, directs, motioning about the room, her voice above the general murmur of conversation. She has no sooner spoken than Dr. Wierwille walks down the stairs into our midst.

"God bless," he greets everyone with a dynamic smile, walking over to his place beside Mrs. Wierwille who is already standing behind her chair. A hush settles over the room.

"Does everybody have seats now?" Dr. Wierwille asks looking around. "All right, let's have the blessing." And he himself launches into it: "Our Father and our God, we thank you for all the work that has been accomplished today to your praise and to your glory. We thank you for blessing this food to the health and strength of our bodies, and we thank you for a great afternoon for everyone, through Christ Jesus, Amen."

Everyone joins in the "Amen" in loud chorus. The room is instantly animated with the sound of scraping chairs, continued conversation and a peel of laughter from Claudettee, who is sitting beside Del and Nancy Duncan on one side and Meg, the artist, on the other. "Now, that is going to be a funny, funny meal," runs through my head, as the banter shifts into high gear.

I really had not even noticed where or with whom I am sitting, but now that I am helping myself to a piece of steaming chicken and passing it on to Doug on my left, I note that at my end of the table Patte Adams, whom we passed by fleetingly at her desk in the Wierwille basement this morning, is our table hostess.

"Charlene, would you start the lima beans, please, and pass them on, and Elena, would you start the water please?" she is saying in a voice both quiet and cool and tinged with a slight Southern lilt. Patte is tall and stately, her curled brown-blonde hair carefully pinned out of her eyes by two small silver barrettes. She takes her duties as a hostess seriously, noting all that is on the table and making sure it is passed around.

"Where are you from in the South, Patte?" I ask her between the salad and the millet.

"From North Carolina," Patte responds. "Would you start the spices and condiments please, Earl?" she adds raising her voice slightly to Earl who is seated farther down the table across from me. "And please keep the spices moving," she admonishes after a minute, as the six little vari-colored shakers — containing regular salt and pepper, red cayenne pepper, green vegetable salt, kelp and capsicum — are forgotten momentarily at the other end of the table. Her hostess responsibilities aside for now, Patte turns back to me.

"I'm from North Carolina," she repeats, and then looking around the table adds, "that's where I met Charlene. We got into the Word together there. And, as a matter of fact, Doug was there too, and Earl. We all got into the Word in North Carolina."

"Isn't it funny that you're all sitting at the same table here at lunch today?" I remark, unable to hide my surprise at the coincidence. For I had been thinking to talk more with each of these people.

"Yes, we hardly see each other; we're all so involved in separate jobs, even though those three are in the Corps, and I'm a W.O.W. ambassador," Doug says joining our conversation.

I leap in with interest. "Did you all get into the Word together? Or how is it you all started there and ended up here?" I toss out a series of questions. All four open their mouths to say something, and then break into a simultaneous laugh.

"I guess you better talk one at a time, so I can hear you," I suggest. "Which of you got into it first?"

"I guess I did," Earl volunteers between bites of food. "I'm from Virginia originally, near Charlottesville; but East

Carolina University is where we all met and heard the Word. I started at ECU in September of 1967 on a football scholarship. I'd been brought up in the Methodist Church and had actually been very active in it. But there were practices I just couldn't see.

"For example, being an officer in the youth program, I got to go to all the board meetings. One time a question came up about buying a piece of property for the church, and one of the board members had an appropriate piece of real estate to sell. Now, you see, my mother was in real estate at that time, and she brought out the fact that the guy wanted a fat price for that land. He was asking a lot more than it was worth. Now, I thought, if his heart is with the church, why doesn't he give it or sell it at a reasonable price? Why jack up the price?

"You see, there were a lot of little things like that that really bugged me — differences between what was taught from the pulpit and what the leaders actually did. There was a whole lot of wheeling and dealing I just couldn't dig. So I was active in it because I didn't know what else to get involved in spiritually, but I had a lot of questions that just weren't answered.

"But anyway, I went away to college at ECU and played football. Sophomore year was pretty good, I played football and got pretty good marks in school; but later that year I got moved from fullback to guard, and that was very hard for me. I was on the first team, but the coach began to blame everything on me. He really began to ride me, and I ended up on the third team in no time. The coach told me I was the worst football player he ever saw, and the law of negative believing began to set in.

"I was pretty disappointed in myself and completely dissatisfied with my situation. That's when a friend of mine told me about the class. But I just wasn't interested. I'd always believed in God, and prayed every night. I often sat down and read the Word, but I just couldn't understand it. Well, a couple of guys told me about the class, but I just wasn't ready, I guess. They said the class was really good, and I said, 'Yeh, Yeh,' but I really didn't mean it.

"After midterms that year, when spring drills started, I made a decision to prove that coach wrong. I decided I'd make the first team and went in with that attitude. Well, the first day of spring drills, I was running and pulled a hamstring. I was injured. That very day was the day the class started. Dr. Wierwille was there to teach it himself.

"I remember the day so well, I was studying and this same friend walked in and said: 'You're coming with me.' I told him 'No, no.' I just wasn't going to go, but then I reconsidered and went with him at the very last minute. I felt weird going in. Dr. Wierwille was teaching and Howard Allen was with him. That was in March of 1969. Doctor taught on positive believing and negative believing. Of course, I'd just seen that principle working in my life on the football team with the coach riding me and my bad performance. Dr. Wierwille was so dynamic and confident. He had all the answers from the Word. I was awed. I was amazed. He captured my attention and after that session I signed up for the rest of the class.

"He taught it live to six people. He told us later that he had been led by God to come here and teach this particular class. I was glad I'd pulled my muscle because the class was more important to me than spring drills. And, because I didn't have the drills, I was alert every night for the class."

Earl pauses in his story, gives us all his dimpled smile, his blue eyes shining with humor under a yellow wave of hair over his forehead. Charlene, Patte and Doug are all listening with rapt interest, and so am I to see the hand of God working in the life of a person.

"The effect of the class was to change my whole attitude," Earl continues. "I could read the Word and understand it. It was what I had been looking for all my life. It blew my mind, but I still wasn't ready to commit myself entirely. After a while, another class came up and I got some people in it. Then the summer came, and there was no fellowship. Everyone went home, but I stayed and went to summer school. Late that summer Howard Allen, Gene Randall and Ira Hearne came to build the Bible Center in Greenville. I hung around them and helped a little. I thought they were the coolest guys I'd ever met.

"That fall, I was divided between football and fellowship, and then one day I saw so clearly that I was sitting on the fence. I saw that I hadn't yet decided to put God first. I saw I had to make up my mind and I decided to commit myself to God.

"Then things really began to happen. In January, 1970, I took the class again, really studied and worked the material. I was believing to get in touch with people, and I started sharing the Word in the dorm. Then other guys started coming. It was really funny how I'd read something in the morning, or go over a certain verse, and that very night someone would ask me about that particular thing. God always gave me the answers beforehand.

"I began to tithe too, and I got a job. There were more and more new people and more fellowships. It blew my mind, and then for the next class in January, 1970, I got 11 or 12 people in. Later that spring Doug here took it too," and Earl directs his gaze at Doug across the table from him.

"Yeh, I was the only long-hair in the ministry then," Doug grins, running his hand in back of his shortly-cropped head. "I had a lot of hassles in my head, but I knew one thing: those people at the fellowship really loved me. I'd never been with people who really loved me before.

"But I wasn't from North Carolina either," Doug corrects. "I went to high school in Florida and spent several summers on Long Island. I started ECU in 1965, but I didn't know where I was going or why, so I got into drugs pretty heavy, pretty fast — grass, acid, mescaline. I didn't study much because I was always spaced out. I went to Puerto Rico, bummed around, did drugs, got a job making a movie. I dropped out of school for a while. I just wasn't going anywhere.

"In January, 1969, I knew I was headed down. I came back to school then, for lack of anything better to do. But I was really tripped out — fearing things. I'd lost all sense of time. I had lost control and was plagued by paranoia. That's when I had a bad trip, and after that I began to fear insanity.

"My brother was in the Word, but I didn't believe anything he said. I used to belittle him, even. One day I prayed that I would believe, but I just couldn't.

"In 1970, about a year after I'd prayed that, I heard some songs by John Lennon and "Jesus Christ — Superstar," and I began to think about it. You see, somewhere, sometime, somehow, someone had told me that before Jesus Christ came back, there would be songs about him, and suddenly I began to think: "Maybe it's all true. Maybe Jesus Christ is going to come back soon." I began to imagine that it was really true, and then I got terribly hungry to know more.

"I asked questions and then I remembered these two guys in my class at ECU who were in The Way, and I knew they had had a class about the Bible. I just knew then and there that I would take it. I knew I had to know more.

"That spring I took the class. That was where I met Earl. I was really filled with the knowledge of God. You see, I wanted to believe. I was ready. I believed the little that I knew, but I knew too little to really share.

"After I had the class I moved into The Way Home. That fall, Earl came back and became the leader of the guys in ECU. We went through a lot of changes together. We had to make beds, keep the place clean. It was hard for me to do those things. But I sure learned a lot." Doug and Earl exchange a knowing glance and smile implying much more than is being voiced.

"That summer I took the Advanced Class out here on the farm. Earl did too and several others from ECU. We had a good group of people standing at ECU then as well as now. North Carolina is not a big area, but people there are strong. Lots of Armed Forces people too. They come to Greenville to have a good time, and we have an opportunity to witness to them. They come looking for something and we just fill that need."

"But how about Charlene and Patte?" I interpose. "How did you two get into it? How did you meet Earl and Doug?" I am curiously awaiting to hear an account of how God brought these individuals from such a variety of situations together.

"We met each other before we met Doug," Charlene begins to recount. She was the girl we saw cleaning film in the Main Office trailer this morning. Petite in build with soft, large eyes like a friendly doe, she talks excitedly about how she and Patte met.

"I'm from Maryland, was raised a Roman Catholic, but I became a Christian my senior year in high school. My mother had died of cancer. And later I had broken up with my boyfriend and was in a lot of mental anguish. I cried out to God, and a month later I got saved through Young Life, a high school Christian group. But I couldn't use any power to renew my mind. I didn't even know that power was available.

"When I went to college, I was really hungry for Christian fellowship. I rapped the Word, shared, read it every day. But no one in the dorm listened to me. I didn't care what other people thought. That's when I heard of this fundamentalist group on campus. I went once, but they were into a lot of bondage. I couldn't dig it: long skirts, no makeup, very dead crowd. And I needed a foundation I could really depend on. I saw Patte there at that meeting, but I didn't talk to her then. I left the meeting early. I just couldn't relate to those people.

"About a week later I saw Patte sitting near my dorm, and we began talking. From then on we became inseparable. We shared and shared. We prayed together, studied together, did everything together.

"A couple of weeks after that we were both in the grocery store. We both came up with the same thing — let's go back to the fundamentalist meeting. It was that night. The funny thing was that we both knew there was no fellowship for us in that meeting. Yet, the idea to go hit us both — bang — right at the same time. I prayed about it, and I had a real strong feeling to go. We didn't know anything about revelation, but we both knew to go.

"So we did. There was a minister there talking about I Corinthians 13. He said there was no such thing as prophecy or miracles or healing. But I had seen miracles. I had seen healings. I just knew he was wrong.

"Up in a Christian camp the summer before, a bunch of us had talked about prayer faith, seeing a person in perfect health and praying together. One boy's father had been very ill. Six of us decided to pray for him. We got in a circle and all pictured him in perfect health, and we got a 'superrush' while we were praying. The very next day, the boy got a call from his father who had been perfectly healed that night.

"So you see, I just knew miracles still happen. When that minister denied it, I decided to talk to him afterwards. Patte and I went up to him and said that we had seen miracles. Just as we were talking to him, two other guys came up and started talking to him. They showed him some things from Corinthians. There was just so much love and patience in their approach. It really impressed me. Patte and I just sat there and listened.

"One of the guys was Doug Murphy. The minister just had no answers for the things Doug brought up. Finally he said to the minister: 'I think that my teacher knows more than yours.' After that, the minister just kind of disappeared. And then I asked Doug about his teacher. That's when he told us about The Way and Dr. Wierwille and invited us back to The Way Home.

"Patte and I went over. Were we surprised! It was beautiful — big, plush, handsomely furnished. It kind of bothered me because I'd been taught a lot about Christians living poorly. But they showed me from the Word where it says God wants us to prosper and lead a more abundant life.

"Then he taught us about the four crucified with Christ and we got into the Trinity. That was very hard for me to see because I had been raised a Catholic. But I had to agree that it just was not anywhere in the Word. And I began to believe what the Word says. Patte and I were so excited when we left that night." Charlene wiggles in her chair and projects a contagious excitement which Patte picks up.

"Yes, we were so excited because we had agreed there was just no Christian fellowship. And suddenly, here it was. And the very next night we had arranged to go back there and meet them again at the coffee house called the 'Way Inn.' That's when that great healing happened. Remember that, Charlene?'' Patte's eyes sparkle as she speaks.

"Earl probably remembers it the best. He and Doug ministered to the other guy, Gerald," Charlene responds.

"Oh yeh, I'd forgotten all about that," Earl shrugs his shoulders. "But now I remember. That was Gerald Wrenn from the football team. It was Saturday night at the Way Inn. He had broken his collarbone in four or six places and was in a shoulder brace."

"Yes, they came in, and the guy in the shoulder brace was really in pain," Patte wrinkles her forehead in simulation of anguish. "His face was all screwed up and someone was helping him to sit down. Then Earl and Doug went over and talked to him for a few minutes and they all went outside for about twenty minutes. Then they came back in and Gerald had the shoulder brace off and was stretching, laughing, rejoicing. I could hardly believe my eyes. Charlene and I were just so amazed and happy. It was like the first century Church or something," Patte ends up ecstatically. "Do you remember that, Earl?"

"Yes, he'd been hurt that afternoon in the Richmond game. When I saw him, I just went over and talked to him for a few minutes. Then I asked him if he wanted ministering and he said, 'Sure.' So I called Doug out with me. As I ministered, I saw the bones come together and knit up in the name of Jesus Christ. Then we prayed.

"For a second, I saw the bones slipping, but I just disciplined my mind to see them back together again and completely healed. When he took the brace off and moved his shoulder, he had no more pain. I wasn't surprised. I expected it. It's just like Doctor teaches — you pray for rain, be sure to bring your umbrella. I just believed God.

"Then we came back in and sat down. Gerald felt great. He tried to go back and play football the next week, but no one would believe he was healed. Even after they took a second X-ray and didn't find any broken bones, they said it took six weeks to heal. They just refused to believe, so they kicked him off the team rather than let him play," Earl laughs recalling the incident.

"You know, Gerald broke his collarbone again later that year," Doug recalls. "That second time, the bone was protruding under the skin even. He called the Way Home and just asked whoever was there to pray for him. We ministered to him over the phone, and he was healed. He had tremendous believing." Doug shakes his head in conclusion.

"You had quite something going on there," I remark in understatement. "It sounds just like the book of Acts."

"It really was," Patte agrees. "In fact it still is. But then we had tremendous boldness and believing. It's what kept us going. Charlene and I claimed three verses, walked out on them, never doubting. What we lacked in knowledge, we made up for in boldness. The verses were: 'We are more than conquerors,' and 'I can do all things through Christ who strengthens me', and 'Seek ye first the kingdom of God and his righteousness and all else will be added unto you.' We hadn't had the class — we just believed God and walked out on that. It was a very exciting time.

"Anyway, Charlene and I started to go to the Way Home every day after school, and every night we'd go witnessing with the others. We saw miracle after miracle," Patte is breathless from wanting to convey so much so quickly.

"Remember that other time that Gerald ministered to the guy at Chapel Hill?" Doug reminds them of another happening. "You see, we went witnessing one Saturday night in Chapel Hill at the University of North Carolina. That's where Steve Aldridge was going to school — he's the roving ambassador that pulled in with Marcia Faulk today. In one of the dorms at the reception desk downstairs there was a guy who had something wrong with his knee. His crutches were leaning against the wall. Gerald began talking to him, found out that he was supposed to go to the hospital for an operation on Monday.

"After Gerald had talked to him some more, he asked if he wanted ministering. The guy agreed. There was a whole bunch of us believers standing around and unbelievers too. We had merely arranged to meet at this particular dorm before going on home."

"I remember that too," Earl comes in excitedly. "I was reluctant to have Gerald minister because he tended to be flippant. But I just believed for revelation. There were a lot of us standing around, believing with him. Gerald prayed for the cartilage, ligaments and the tendons in the knee to go back together. And while he was praying, he told me later, he had his hand on the guy's knee, and he felt things moving under the knee cap. He could actually feel it all going back into place. While he was praying, I got a picture of all those things going back into order, too."

"What happened then?" I urge him on, leaning over the table toward him wanting to hear more.

"Let me tell you, there was no small stir. There was, in fact, a lot of excitement. The guy took off the bandage, felt his knee. He couldn't believe it. Then he started walking around. No, first he put his full weight on that leg. And then he started walking around. It worked perfectly and he had no pain. And then he began doing deep knee bends and running in place. He pushed the crutches aside. He had no pain at all.

"He was so amazed he couldn't believe that he could be-lieve. He started calling people on the intercom, telling every-one he talked to that he had been healed. Or people who walked in. He just told every single person there: 'I'm healed. I'm healed.' He never had his operation the next week, but he split for Florida shortly after that. We haven't heard from him. But that miracle surely built us all up. Even though some people who watched the whole thing never believed at all." Earl winds up the story, Patte, Charlene and Doug all bubbling around him.

"I haven't thought of that all in a long time," Patte muses quietly. "But it seems things like that were just going on all the time, every day. We were higher than kites — all of us. That was in October. By November, Charlene and I both quit school and took the class. My parents took it pretty hard when I left school because I was brought up to get married, and college was the place to find a good husband. They couldn't understand that I wanted to do God's will full-time rather than memorize men's knowledge. And here we all are in the Way Corps and Doug W.O.W., all doing God's work, getting ready to do more." Patte comes to a stop, just as a peel of laughter from Claudettee, Meg and Del momentarily drowns out my thoughts.

"That must have been a good one." Charlene giggles at their laughter, and the coffee pot makes a second pass from one to another of us following the conversation. The plates are littered with ravaged chicken bones. Everyone at our table is sitting back, relaxed, full. Listening to these stories of the old days throughout lunch, I have hardly been aware of the stir, the general looseness, the joyous atmosphere around me.

I start to replay their accounts through my mind. It's true, they were all in college, all in the same college, but each one on such a different trip: drugs, football, religion or brought up to get married. Yet darkness is darkness, whatever its shape, form or flavor. And God meets such a variety of needs, reaches out to people where they are. No matter what darkness we are in, and we were all in it, God delivers us from a dark womb of the world into the light of His Word.

*The Wierwille farm before 1961*

*The sign at the state Route 29*

*Dr. Wierwille and Mr. Pupala, Mayor of Bombay, India in 1955*

*Dr. Wierwille as he appears today*

*Morning run—The Way Corps—Morning prayer group*

*Flag raising*

*Del and Nancy Duncan
helping celebrate son
Aaron's second birthday.*

*Visitors arrive frequently at The Way Headquarters*

*The bridge across the River Jordan*

*Preparing home-cooked meals*

*Announcements after dinner—Mrs. Wierwille standing*

*Tina Ranyak—offset press*

*Fred Wilson—Printing department*

## Just another day at The Way

*Danny Shroyer—mailing*

*Sue Wilson astride April Day*

*Bob Wierwille, Howie Yeremian (with camera), Tim Bishop*

*Lonnell Johnson at light table*

*Gary Curtis translating studies in Spanish*

*Linda Filbrun
Bookstore*

*Brenda Warren and
Lonnell at campfire*

*Happy Birthday!
(into the pond!)*

*Original W.O.W. Ambassadors (hand symbol represents "Word Over the World")*

*Camp discussion—Dr. Wierwille, Dr. Peter J. Wade, Jan George and Dorothy Owens*

*Witnessing—Gail and Frances Winegarner, Ambassadors-at-large and Marcia Faulk, Ambassador-on-wheels*

*Meg Watson at the map in the Dining Room (Photo courtesy of Toledo Blade)*

*Pool game in the Wierwille basement*

*Everyone joins in baseball games*

*Dr. Wierwille teaching*

*Children at Rock of Ages '71 led by Ted Ferrell*

*Rock of Ages '71*

*Gary Curtis at the Rock of Ages '71*
*portraying Peter on the day of Pentecost*

*Dr. Wierwille's office on the film set*

*Making the class film in 1967. Left to right—Emogene Allen, Howard Allen, Max Kent, Dr. Wade, Donna Randall*

*Some of Dr. Wierwille's family: Back row center, Dr. Wierwille; to the right is Mrs. Wierwille, sister Lydia, daughter Sara, sister Sevilla. To the left is brother Harry, son John, Harry's wife, Naomi  Front row, left to right: daughter Karen, Amy and Matthew (Mary's children) and daughter Mary*

*The Way Biblical Research Center*

*Aerial view of The Way Headquarters*

Across my thoughts, a hush spreads through the room, and I turn to see Dr. Wierwille perched on the back of his black chair, and ready for the announcements. After meals there is always a time for announcements or sharing — for me one of the most precious times of the day.

"Well, are there any announcements today?" Dr. Wierwille questions in his vibrant voice. No response. "Anybody got anything to share?" Again no response. He looks around the dining room, meeting the eyes of one person after another. "Well, whatcha been doing all morning? I guess nothing's happening today," and he gives us his quick peel of laughter.

"All right then, I'll just share with you. How's that?" he proposes emphatically, enunciating every word. His eyes squeezed shut, he seems to concentrate for a long time. Everyone waits in anticipation, for when Doctor is relaxed and sharing after lunch or after supper, the wonderful spirit and love of one big family is so thick and sweet that it can be touched and felt. It's as though he just opens up his heart and lets us all walk right in, all of us. He does not hold anything back, thereby putting each one of us in a privileged and special position of being trusted, valued and loved. You see, he has lots of things to do, decisions to make, letters to write, people to see; but he cares enough to take the time to share with us. And that is a priceless honor.

"There were two men in Van Wert," he begins slowly. "Now, they got together every morning at 5 a.m. and believed together for an hour. Every morning. I don't know what they called it. But they would set their minds on an agreed project. They never spoke; just got together every morning and both concentrated on whatever it was, until it came to pass.

"Oh, they both belonged to some local church, I guess. They paid their $50 or $100 a year, or whatever, but they never went to church, or hardly ever, anyways.

"I remember they got involved in Cuba some time ago, in sugar. That was before all the changes in Cuba. After a while, they had so much sugar, they decided they needed a distillery to use up that sugar for the most profit.

"Well, they just got together and put their minds on it every single morning for a couple of weeks, and lo and behold, one day suddenly some guy who wanted to sell his distillery just called them up, asked if they wanted to buy it. They'd never heard of the guy with the distillery before. He found them.

"Yep, they made millions, gambled, won. One man set up a foundation for children from broken homes, also built the YMCA, YWCA and a hospital. It was something." Dr. Wierwille pauses in the expectant stillness, shuts his eyes tightly again, and, after a few moments' pause, goes on.

"I used to watch how they operated. I was a minister there in Van Wert. I had my church, my congregation. But I studied them. That was before God showed me the law of believing in all its accuracy. You see, here were the two meanest guys you could ever want to meet. Nobody liked them because they were so successful and no one else could hold a candle to them.

"I used to look at their successes — one after another — and then I'd look at those defeated Christians all around me. And I was just amazed. I just couldn't understand it, until I understood from the Word of God the law of believing, the greatest law in the world today. Then I could see just what was happening.

"It says in Mark that whosoever — now what does whosoever mean? Whosoever means whosoever, not just Christians, not just Catholics, not just Way believers, but 'Whosoever shall say unto this mountain, Be thou removed, and be thou cast into the sea; and shall not doubt in his heart, but shall believe that those things which he saith shall come to pass; he shall have whatsoever he saith.' There it is, spelled out, the greatest law there is.

"Now, I don't know if those guys ever looked at the Word of God. I doubt it. But they knew that law. They operated it, and sure made it work for them. They used it for money, for their profit — not for the glory of God — and that law worked for them.

"Just picture such believing to do God's work, to get the accuracy and integrity of God's Word over the world. Just think of operating that law to do God's will, with all the power of God in you. Boy, it can't fail.

"Our believing in the Word of God just has to get to that point where those two guys got it, so that we can move with the Word of God the way they moved in their business. Do you see it? Do you see it?" Doctor looks around the room, his hands extended before him as though he were showing or offering us something, something to grasp with our believing.

"Now those guys had disciplined minds. We all need discipline, and you have got to get it while you're here. You have to do it now." He makes the point and then sighs thoughtfully.

"I've been talking the last couple of days with the men working on the campaign in California. We're working it out. We'll begin on April 2 in Oakland, California. We'll be running there five nights, a real tight program with music, teaching from the Word of God for 45 minutes, then making the 'Power for Abundant Living' Class available.

"If it works, if we can draw in the people, then we'll go on to other cities. I'm prepared for the next 18 months to do that, one week per month, anywhere in the country, but only if we are able to reach people this way. It's not a one-man trip, but it's The Way, it's all your believing with it that's going to make this thing jell.

"After Oakland, I go to Rye, New York, for three weeks to teach the Advanced Class there. So I'm not going to be around much the next six weeks. But it's here that the strength of the ministry stands. It will take an effort on everybody's part here. But you and I know it's the Word. God is our strength. It's not VP Wierwille's trip. It's the Body, wherever a believer is, he's part of the Body.

"And you're my kids. You're just the greatest." His voice breaks momentarily, his forehead wrinkles, his eyes red with tears of tenderness, he holds back nothing from us. And we — we are all moved, touched to the core by his sharing his emotion with us.

Not allowing his emotion to take mastery over him, he continues after a short pause, picking up his earlier thought.

"I've been talking to these men in California lately. They earn about $250,000 a year. They are tops in business, in advertising. But what can you do with all that money? Can you buy health? Can you buy happiness? What's all that money worth? What is anything worth without God?

"One of these men, he's got so much money, but he's going to be a dead man within five years if he doesn't go with God. He's being eaten away by fears and worries. All that money just can't buy peace in the heart. If it were my choice, I'd go with God." He laughs deep inside, his eyes filling with tears.

"It's the Word. It's the Word. If God didn't give us His Word, then there's just nothing left to live for. But when you know that Word and work it, you get the results. And you know what? It doesn't hurt anybody. Love or peace or joy or healing just never hurt anybody. Don't let anyone ever touch the Word. Because it's truth, and that stands whatever happens." He stops, looks around, smiles at us all, and then seems to shift to a new vein, practical, businesslike.

"This campaign is really going to be something. We'll all learn. We've never tried it before. We may have a thousand in the first class — now, that's what I've been working on. Running it through my brain. What's the best way to run a class of that size? Is it better to have one person with four helpers run a class of forty-four and have 20 small classes, or to have two classes of five hundred?

"I may call all the Corps and all the ambassadors into Oakland. We need leaders, people who are disciplined, spiritually on top of it. We don't need anyone who is satisfied with a four- to six-hour day. I need people out there who can stay on top through a twenty-hour day, then wake up the next morning refreshed and be on top of it for another twenty-hour day. Day after day.

"You got to be ready," the humor and the old fight in the face of a great challenge are back in his tone of voice. "You've got to be ready because you're all I've got. If you aren't ready, who is going to run those classes, undershepherd those people, teach others to stand and lead?" The question hangs over us in mid-air. The answer is obvious. God is our strength. We are built-up, encouraged, ready, for God is our strength.

"All right now, are there any announcements? I've talked enough. I want to hear you talk now." Dr. Wierwille laughs warmly and throws the meeting open to everyone else. A few hands go up.

"OK, Craig," Doctor calls his name, and Craig stands up holding a letter in his hand.

"Here's an incident I wanted to share with you all today. It came in yesterday in one of the W.O.W. weekly reports. It's from our W.O.W. ambassador in Fort Wayne, Indiana. He says that one of the people in the fellowship broke his collarbone last week. He works in a warehouse or something, and some stuff he was loading fell on him. They took an X-ray and saw the crack. He was believing to be completely healed.

Two days later he went back to the doctor who took another X-ray. The doctor said it was impossible. He couldn't understand it, so they took a third X-ray. It was completely healed. So he's back at work," Craig concludes. Everyone is laughing, rejoicing. A loud burst of applause fills the dining room.

"I just thought you'd enjoy hearing that," Craig grins and sits down.

"All right, Doug." Doctor chooses someone else.

"I got a good letter yesterday, too," Doug begins, standing up beside me. "From a brother in North Carolina with a few more details about the parachute accident we all lifted last week. Apparently, the guy we were lifting jumped first. It was a free fall. But another guy jumped too soon after him, fell on top of him, breaking his arm so that he couldn't pull his parachute open. He fell 1800 feet to the ground. The parachute never opened, but tangled up because he couldn't pull the cord. He broke both thighs and punctured a lung, as well as breaking his arm.

"Anyway, in this letter my friend said that his lung is completely healed. He's still in traction in the hospital, but he's back to his old self, laughing and kidding around. He's praising God that he's alive today. He's positive that if it hadn't been for God's grace, he'd have been killed. So he's in great spirits, glorifying God, witnessing to everyone that comes near his bed, and believing to be out of the hospital real soon. And he thanks us all for our prayers," Doug finishes to another burst of applause.

"Who would like to drop him a line," Craig calls, and

someone else responds: "Let's tell him to drop in here sometime." Another round of guffaws. Everyone loves to laugh.

"All right, Mark, go ahead. You told me before lunch that
you had an announcement. Let's hear it." Doctor calls on the
red-bearded, long-haired young man in the faded jumpsuit,
we saw collecting the garbage with Randy this morning. Mark
is an audio engineer by profession, who works with musical
groups here on the farm when necessary. He spent some time
here this winter, and yesterday arrived for a short stay from
New York. Mark hesitates, then stands up slowly, clearing his
throat.

"Well, I see I'm on," Mark begins. "And I see that, even if
you change your mind you're stuck with an announcement if
you let anyone know beforehand that you have an announcement." Everyone is laughing already, knowing Mark's knack
for coming up with stories.

"I came back here from New York yesterday. I'm real glad
to be back because the food is just great here. I was walking
around the streets of New York, and you know something?
I've become a country boy. I just do everything slow and
easy now. I just rejoiced in what was here on the farm. It's so
terrific and there's just no place like it in the world. I was so
blessed that I could spend some time here. But you know
what I saw most of all? Great as it is to be here, it's good it
won't be forever. Because there's just so much to be done out
there in the world. Praise God. There's such a need out there
to hear the Word. We just got to get all we can here, and then
get out into the world and start spreading it." Mark pauses.

It's like a breeze in the window to hear a comment from someone just back from the outside.

"Well, I guess I had an announcement after all. But I didn't know it was going to turn into a teaching. Anyway, I'm real glad to be here because I love you all a lot. I spent a couple of weeks in New York, and some fantastic things happened to me, but I won't tell you yet, till I talk to Uncle Harry.

"I tell you, New York was great, and God really protected me every minute. And you know what? I want to tell you, the same God who protected me in New York was protecting Randy and me all morning while we were collecting the garbage. We gotta figure out what to do with the aerosol cans in the garbage, because when we burn the garbage, we toast marshmallows on the fire, and those cans explode. So we'll have to do something about it, and then we'll invite you all to come out and toast marshmallows with us."

Everyone is cracking up around him for Mark is a natural clown. "Well, that's it. I sure love you all. It's great to be back and God bless you." Mark sits down.

The laughter subsides and Doctor calls next on Paul Vergilio. Thick brown locks cover his head. His face is accented by a handsome handlebar mustache and two lively, flashing eyes. He is the leader of the folk rock singing group, Selah, of Way Productions. The group consists of five members, four men and lovely Kristina, the female vocalist. Besides playing at Sunday night meetings here and at teen clubs, dances, concerts, and festivals in the area, Selah is currently cutting its first album of groovy Christian sounds.

An orphan from Italy who grew up in Philadelphia to success as a song writer and guitarist in California, Paul speaks in short, to-the-point phrases.

"I just wanna say, that the love of God was with us all the way yesterday in the studio. All the way. Compared to what we went in with, what we came out with was so much better than we had even hoped for. So we all know that God was right there with us. It was great. We finished all the instrumentals in one day, and we've got the vocals left. We'll be finishing them up this week and next. Praise the Lord. I want you all to know how great and helpful Ted and Mardelle Ferrell were. They worked closely with us all the way. I know you were all lifting us, too. So thanks for your prayers." Paul sits down.

"All right, Eddie, what do you want to tell us?" Doctor calls on Selah's other male vocalist.

"I just wantta say, we need someone to teach tonight at the Urbana fellowship. They're a great bunch of really turned on kids. Paul and I have been teaching there every week, but we gotta be at the studio in Cincinnati tonight. Is there someone who'll teach there?" Eddie isn't finished with his sentence before Tim's hand is up at another table.

"Thanks, Tim. They're a great bunch of kids. Tell them we love them all, and that we'll be back after we're through recording."

"All right, Tina, what've you got for us?" Doctor points to someone else.

"I want everyone to know," Tina begins and falters in a little giggle as she stands up, "that Claudettee and Beth Ricks got their licenses today."

"Their marriage licenses?" Doctor comes back. There's a wave of laughter.

"No, no, their drivers' licenses," Tina clarifies above the laughter.

"All right, Dave Anderson," Doctor moves right on, and Dave stands up.

"I wanted all of you to know that we have four film classes running right now: Toledo, Alameda, California — they both have thirty- five in them — and Smithtown, Long Island. And they're getting ready to open up a tape class in Hawaii next week. I forgot where the other film class is running."

"All right, Doug again."

"I'd like to see all the members of the Rock of Ages planning committee right after supper in the fireplace room. We need to go over some plans."

"Very good. Someone else. Earl."

"Remember, there's a class starting here on the farm in three days. Anyone you talk to, remind them of it. And the class Dave forgot to mention is the Miamisburg class outside of Dayton. It has twenty-four people in it, and it's running beautifully." Earl finishes with an enthusiastic smile and sits down.

"Craig, you have another announcement?"

"I just wanted to remind everyone that we'll be having prayer at ten of one, right after lunch upstairs in the Bible Center, to continue to lift the things of the ministry."

"Who's next. Patte, what've you got, honey?"

"I've done all the sewing and mending that was left on my machine, so all you fellas, you know who you are, that left things there can come and pick up your stuff."

"Well, I thought nothing happened today," Doctor admonishes us lovingly, "and look at all the announcements. I guess I warmed you up. Boy, this mustache sure itches," he remarks scratching his mustache that he grew two weeks ago. "If it goes on itching, she's comin' off."

"That means you're coming into some money," Meg pipes up from her seat beside Mrs. Wierwille. "That's what it means: If your mustache itches you'll come into some money soon."

"Oh, I don't know. How do women get any money if they don't have mustaches?" Doctor laughs. "I don't know, girl. But I hope that's revelation. Anyone else? All right, Brenda."

The sweet smiling black girl from Washington, D.C. who was working in the Main Office trailer this morning, stands at her seat.

"I wanted to let you all know what happened to my grandmother. I asked you all to pray for her two days ago because there had been a severe flood down in the area of West Virginia where she lives. Well, my mother called me today to say she'd heard from my grandmother, and even though the flood was all around her and her house, it just didn't get to her. She's just fine. Praise the Lord." Brenda finishes radiantly.

"Well, God's still in business," Doctor comments. "OK, Pat Johnson. What is it, son?"

"I want to remind all staff members and guests that there'll be a twig fellowship tonight after supper at my home in Trailer 8. It's going to be a sharing kind of fellowship, and it's going to be just great. Everyone will get blessed. See you all there, tonight after supper."

"All right. The staff's having a twig fellowship tonight. That's fine. You know, I think the Corps is going to go witnessing tonight. I'll just think it over this afternoon and tell you tonight at supper. All right. I'm glad I thought of that. It's about time you all got out for a while.

"Anyone else? Mrs. Wierwille, you go ahead and have yourself a good announcement," Doctor encourages affectionately.

"I want to remind you all to clean up and wash up at night after those late snacks. You know, these two refrigerators are for you to eat from and snack from. No one is to go into the walk-in or the freezers. But after you've had your snacks, clean up; otherwise we'll just have to disallow any bedtime snacks. The cooks come in early in the morning and find the sink and counter full of dishes. That's just not fair. If you eat late at night, clean up. OK. I'm through." Mrs. Wierwille smiles at us after the sharpness of her reproof. We know she loves us, even though we need to be corrected sometimes.

The announcements trickle to a stop. Doctor looks around again.

"Anyone else before Nancy reads the honor roll?" he questions, looking around. The honor roll is the list of five people who do dishes after supper, because the cooks and kitchen help leave by five. With so many here, a name comes up about once a week. Four wash dishes and one man scrubs the kitchen floor. But Bo's hand is up very straight above his head.

"I have an announcement but for after the dishes list," he tells us mysteriously.

"All right, Nancy, let's hear the dishes list so we can get to Bo's surprise. If it comes after dishes it's going to be good, I betcha." Doctor opens his eyes round and wide, raising his eyebrows meaningfully.

Nancy begins reading: "On dishes tonight we have Brenda, Susan Wilson, Dave Buschman, Nicholas and Sky Wood on the floor." She reads the last name and everyone claps for the clean-up crew.

"Now Bo, let's have yours. I'm curious." Doctor's curiosity shows all over his face, open as a child's on Christmas morning. Bo stands up slowly. Everyone is sitting forward in anticipation.

"Today is a very special day for all of us, and a specially important day for one special person." He pauses and looks around the room. We hold our breaths, waiting for the news. "It's Earl's birthday!" Bo announces after the build-up, and with one accord the room bursts into a loud "Happy Birthday" in four-part harmony. Earl stands up blushing from the roots of his wavy blond hair across his forehead down to the collar of his flowered shirt. The second verse of the Happy Birthday song goes: "God's blessings on you, God's blessings on you." Everyone joins in full voice to a dramatic, harmonic crescendo which dissolves into whistling and applause.

But Bo is still standing. There must be more to come, and a hush falls quickly over the crowd. Bo continues, "Since it is a special day for Earl today, and since he is the branch leader of the Miami Valley Branch here in Ohio, we here at The Way International Headquarters have a very special gift to present to him. Howie, would you go into the next room and prepare to present the gift to Earl?" Bo and Howie simulate a diplomatic formality. Someone else simulates the roll of drums. Earl looks toward the door expectantly, and then Howie emerges holding aloft a huge winter branch, tied about with a shiny yellow bow.

It's a hit. The room explodes at the wit and insight behind the gift. But Earl is nonplussed.

"How about accepting it, Earl?" Mrs. Wierwille suggests. Howie smiling, strides melodramatically in Earl's direction meeting him in the center of the floor. They shake hands. Earl reaches to take the gift with his left hand and then draws it back suddenly.

"Wait a minute. We all learned the Orientalism behind the right and left hands. I have to take it with my right hand because that's the hand of blessing, the left is the hand of cursing. A gift is always given and accepted in the right hand." Earl stops talking and takes it correctly, holding its prickly twigs and thorns away from his face. A chorus of "Speech, speech," rises up, and Earl clears his throat. A silence falls as suddenly as it was lost.

"This is the finest gift I have ever gotten in my life. What I see here among the twigs is some thorns. But fortunately, not all the twigs have thorns. This is a branch from a sycamore tree, by the way.

"Well, it's just great. There's only one thing wrong with this branch, and that is it has no leaves. As you all know, a branch without leaves cannot live. Also, it's broken off from the trunk. I'm going to do all I can, I'll probably use trunk to trunk resuscitation to revitalize it. Or maybe I'll just graft it on to Reverend Cummins' desk," Earl finishes, grinning broadly, and sits down to loud cheers and applause with his newly-acquired branch.

Everyone is full of uninhibited gaiety. Birthdays are always celebrated here: in the summer by a toss into the pond; at other times with cake and candles, and always by singing and congratulations. It's just like a family. In fact, it is a family — God's children together in the household of God.

"I guess that's it, everybody." Doctor is addressing us all again in his warmly vibrant voice, relaxed and carefree after a good laugh.

"I'm sure glad something is happening here today. When I called for them, there were no announcements. I guess it takes you guys a while to warm up. OK, let's roll it away. Have a great afternoon and God bless. See you all at supper." Doctor eases himself off the back of his chair and strides toward the steps. He stops to talk to two or three people individually, a hug for this one, a hand on the shoulder of another. He is free, not holding back encouragement, recognition or love.

That's how lunches are, full of fellowship. One body, one spirit. Doctor pauses momentarily by my seat. Above the clanging, scraping and tinkling of dishes being cleared away and piled, he addresses me.

"You got time this afternoon?" he inquires. I nod without hesitation. "Then let's you and me go for a ride today. I'll see you at the car in ten minutes." And he is gone.

I pass along the remaining dishes, rejoicing at the occasion. Many days I have sat in the Doctor's office, attended his Way Corps and Sunday night teachings, have sat in on his meetings, his telephone conversations — to see the work, to see the man. But he rarely has much time, uninterrupted by appointments or phone calls, to answer questions, to talk of himself, his life, his early ministry.

It is not every day that I get to go for a ride with Doctor Wierwille, to have his uninterrupted attention for a few hours. The questions formulate in my mind. I want to hear it all, to know his stand. I want to see his soul. He told me that one day he would take me to the places where his search into the Word of God began. This is the day. Thrilled with anticipation, I quickly excuse myself to pick up my notebook before joining him at the car.

The long blue Oldsmobile "98" is parked outside the Wierwille home. I am ready. The sky has settled into a threatening gray cast, the clouds so low and thick even the fierceness of the rising wind does not blow them away. The coldness of winter has gripped the land again, reluctant to release its grasp. I recall the redness of the morning sunrise. Perhaps it will snow, like that little blizzard we had a few days ago.

But although winter blusters importantly in the air, the subtle signs of spring are unmistakable, irrevocable. Along the winding creek, the pussy willows have already sprung out — brown, fuzzy bumps on thick red stalks. The branches of the surrounding bushes are bright yellow, orange, purple and red, flowing with the juice of awakening life. Two swallows dart through the air, like silver birds against a gray sky, in and out of the sheep fence which lines the road. They fill the air with incessant twittering. Unfooled by the frowning sky, they carry bits of straw and dead branches to build their nest high under the eve of the Snack Shoppe.

Doctor Wierwille emerges from the house, striding purposefully to the car. He has left behind his faded work clothes of the morning's tasks, replacing them with an emerald green shirt, accented by a wide tie in yellow and shades of green, brown slacks and a beige military-styled raincoat with epaulettes and high-back belt. I note again how he dresses always appropriately and with an elegant flair.

We climb into the car, cruise slowly down the driveway. A glimpse in the door of the Biblical Research Center reveals two dozen people seated on the floor. It's the prayer time after lunch. Individuals here and there are headed back to their places of work for the afternoon. Everything will continue without us — the Way Corps in afternoon study hall, the Print Shop, the Main Office, the cleaning, construction, collating, working the grounds — everything will continue here according to the order, but we are on a trip through the past.

"Well, what's on your heart?" Dr. Wierwille asks me. "What do you want to know?" Unbothered by phone calls, people, and the press of immediate decisions, he is free to answer questions. My head is still at dinner — the miracles, the healings in North Carolina, the parachute jumper who fell

1800 feet and lived, the man with the broken collarbone. My mind is still thrilling at these events.

"I bet in your years of ministering you've seen some fantastic healings," I venture. "Can you tell me about some of them?"

Doctor Wierwille drives looking at the road straight ahead of him. He says nothing for a long time. Then turning to me with a tender and compassionate smile, he finally answers.

"I don't remember too many specific healings. You see," he searches for words to explain, "healings and miracles are a result of the Word of God living in a person's heart or living in the midst of a group of people. Healings and miracles are by-products of the Word.

"You remember when Jesus sent out the seventy, giving them power to heal the sick and cast out devils? They returned rejoicing at how the power worked; but Jesus told them not to get carried away by the power they had, but to rejoice that their names were written in heaven.

"There's another scripture in the Gospels where Jesus was teaching the multitudes. Do you know what He was teaching? Yes, the Word of God. It says He taught the multitudes, and they were all healed. That must have been really something. He taught the Word and they were *all* healed. Not one was left out. The Word of God heals. It's nothing to be amazed at. When the Word lives, people are healed. You don't dwell on it; you just go on with God's work.

"That's renewed mind — you don't carry any leftovers in your mind — good or bad. Let me tell you something. Seventy people took the last Advanced Class exam. Forty-four got into the class. For two or three weeks I have these names in my head. I lift them every day. By the time I hit that class, I'll have every name firmly in my head. I just lift them all. By the second night of the class, I'll know every face, and I'll put every face and name together.

"The human mind is sure a fantastic thing. After the class is over, I don't carry them with me anymore. I just put in the people that are going to be in the next class.

"When you're in this ministry, the past is the past. You just have to leave it behind. It's always an eternal *now*. When I come into my office in the morning, it's a new day. That's in the renewed mind. It doesn't matter about yesterday, or the number of healings performed yesterday. It's enough to deal with what's happening now, at any time. God doesn't take thoughts away from you. You have to have the ability to shift from one thing to another instantaneously. The human mind is so fantastic. It can do that.

"But I never forget a scripture. I keep certain scriptures in my mind until I have them worked out. Then I drop them out too. I think of the verses to which I don't have the answer. There's one on my desk now. It's been there for the last six years. It's the problem of the two possessing devils in Mark 8 and 9. But that'll fall into place too." Doctor pauses, looking at the road ahead of him.

"Well, I'm here to talk with you. I want to take you to Payne, where I had my first church, and Van Wert, where I ministered for thirteen years. I want to show you those places. I want to open my heart to you. I'll tell you everything you want to know if it'll add any light to understanding my life."

"Start at the beginning," I propose the obvious. "How did God talk to you?"

"OK, I'll start at the beginning. But people just won't believe." He shakes his head wistfully. We speed past great expanses of corn and bean fields, standing empty and brown. But now and again, tender green clusters are visible between the furrows, new growth amid the dead stalks of last year's crops. Under the overcast sky a few stray snowflakes melt on the windshield.

"I was born on December 31, 1916, right in the kitchen of the house we live in now. It was my grandma's farm then, but my father ran it. He had everything — cattle, hogs, horses, all kinds of vegetables and grain. I don't remember much. A tornado blew away my sister Lydia's place when I was about three, and she came back to live with us for a while during the time they were rebuilding their house. Ask her about it, sometime. I just remember the event, but not much else.

"I have 'two brothers and two sisters living and one brother and one sister dead. Brother Otto, the oldest, was killed in a car accident in Lima. I remember it, but that was much later.

"The next thing I recall vividly happened when I was eight or nine years old. There was a Mission Festival in New

Knoxville. I was sitting with my mother. (The men and women sat separately in those days.) There was a guest minister that day, a certain Dr. Lohman, and after the sermon — I don't remember much of what he said — we went up to meet him. We shook hands, you know, and he asked me what I wanted to be. I told him, 'A man of God like you.' That's what I said, but I thought it was just kid's talk. You know how kids talk.

"I guess I grew up like most of the kids around these parts. I went to a one-room school house until sixth grade and then to the New Knoxville School where I finally graduated.

"I flunked algebra, you see. I was a C student until my junior year in high school. That's when I got expelled. The only reason I went back was because of my sister Sevilla. She talked to me. She just kept talking, until she talked me into going back. I was never going to go back.

"I flunked algebra because that algebra teacher, the superintendent, didn't like me. He knew my older brother, Otto, and didn't like him. So when I came along, he just transferred his dislike of Otto to me. He bugged me. He told me he had expelled me because I never would amount to anything. I really disliked him. If I had met him behind a building sometime, I think I would have let him have it. He made me that mad.

"After that, I thought to myself: I'll show him. So it really worked out for the best. When I went back to school after that expulsion, I was determined. I worked hard and became a good student.

"There's only one man I disliked so intensely as I disliked that superintendent, and that was the man who killed my brother Otto in the car accident. He was a black man, and after that I disliked black people for a long time. It took me years to get over it." Doctor pauses to make a turn, and then starts on a new track.

"I got my first motorcycle when I was a sophomore in high school. My brother Reuben and I got it together. It was a one-cylinder job — you had to run along beside it to get it started. We used to take turns riding that thing.

"And I used to play the guitar in those days. Two guys and I had a group together. We'd play and sing at dances and parties. But do you know something? I felt embarrassed about it, or something. So one day in high school, I just put that guitar in its case and I never took it out again. I brought 'her' with me to college even. I loved that guitar, but I just never played it again.

"And my wife, Dotsie, I knew her when we were children together. We used to sit together in church every Sunday because our mothers knew each other and would sit together. Her mother didn't believe in eating in church, but my mother always brought crackers. So Dotsie would get to eat my mother's crackers in church. Maybe that's why I married her, to get back at her for all those crackers of my mother's that she ate in church when we were little," and he laughs warmly.

"The other thing I liked to do was to play basketball. I was offered a scholarship to play basketball at Ohio State University after high school. But my father said no. He wanted me to go to Mission House College in Sheboygan, Wisconsin. He said, 'That's where we've contributed money, that's where you go.' It's religiously affiliated, now called Lakeland College. It used to be Evangelical and Reformed, but now it's United Church of Christ.

"I always knew I wanted to help people. First, I thought I wanted to be a doctor, then a lawyer; but by my junior year in college, I had my heart set on the ministry.

"I played basketball all through college and was even involved in the pro-team, the Sheboygan Redskins. Dotsie and I were married the summer of 1937. She had just finished her nursing degree. We kept the marriage a secret for the next six months, so that I could still play basketball. She came up to Sheboygan with me and worked as a nurse while I finished my studies.

"The favorite men who taught me in Lakeland were Dr. Hessert, Dr. Beckman, Dr. Ernst, Dr. Friedli, Dr. Bauer, the first philosopher I knew — he was a favorite professor of mine, took a real interest in me. Dr. Ernst taught me German. Most of these are no longer living. At the University of Chicago Divinity School there were Dr. Riddle, Dr. Weiman, Dr. William Warren Sweet, Dr. Garrison, and Dr. Caldwell. They were the best minds in their fields — fine men.

"I went to Princeton Theological Seminary in 1940. Donnie was born that summer, and we moved to Princeton that September so I could get my Master's Degree in Practical Theology. Dotsie worked as a nurse during that time. I guess it was a typical grad-student situation. I don't remember much now. The professors I had were the tops in their areas — Dr. Blackwood, Dr. Loetcher, Dr. Homrichhausen, the Niebuhr brothers, Richard and Rhinehold. I heard them all, had the full seminary trip.

"I did everything. I was always a prolific reader, and I read everything I could get a hold of on theology and all that stuff. At Princeton I did my dissertation on Peter as a young man of promise, Peter as evangelist and pastor.

"I don't remember much of the past. I'll have to renew my mind. Oh yes, did I tell you I taught at Gordon Divinity School? Homiletics was my specialty — that's preaching. I took everything I could take at the Moody Bible Institute too, through their correspondence courses.

"And in the years that followed, there were many men I learned from: Glenn Clark, Karl Barth from Switzerland, E. Stanley Jones, Paul Tillich, Starr Daily, Rufus Mosley, Dr. John Gaynor Banks, and there were many, many others. I tried to get all I could learn from anybody.

"When I graduated from Princeton, I got my first church in Payne, Ohio. We're going to be there soon, and you'll see it. I had written to a couple of places in this area of Ohio, and the church in Payne invited me to pastor.

"We came here in June of 1941, right after I was ordained. I guess I started with youth and enthusiasm. But I was very discouraged fast. I'd had the best education money could buy, but with all that I knew, I just could not help people. It just didn't bring people peace and joy, or the accuracy and integrity of God's Word.

"I was very discouraged the first year in the ministry. I prayed a great deal about it. Even then I was discouraged with my life. The principles of the ministry bothered me. The shallowness bothered me.

"The people in my congregation in Payne were prosperous and very sensitive on money. When I got there, the elders called me in and told me I had the run of the pulpit, and that I could teach on anything as long as I never mentioned money. That first fall, for four Sundays in a row I taught on tithing, but I didn't once mention money. And they called me down, right in the basement of the church, and really sounded off at me.

"You see, it was that shallowness that so discouraged me. We'll go this far and no further. That's how they looked at it. God has a place in this building for an hour a week. That's how far we'll go and no further, even if it is God's Word." A long silence hovers between us.

"I remember Pearl Harbor. When was it? December of 1941? I debated that day what to do as a minister. Where do I stand now that my country is at war? Do I enlist? I decided I'd do a greater service to my country by staying home and serving as a minister here.

"I remember that decision. I guess it was that kind of thinking, that kind of soul searching, that kind of deep concern that brought me to the date in August. I was writing monthly articles for a religious publishing firm in Indiana — Higley's. I was there in Indiana when I met a lady who had just returned from years in the mission field in China. Her name was Rosalind Rinker.

"She had been in missionary work in the Far East for many years, and she herself had been converted by another woman named Alleta Jacobs who on her return to the United States had her ship bombed and had died in the sinking of the ship. I never met Alleta Jacobs before she died, but she must have been some woman.

"After I met Rosalind Rinker in Indiana, I invited her to visit us in Payne, and she came for a week that summer of 1942. Maybe it was August. I remember it was near the end of summer, and she used to dog me on the Bible being the Word of God. She talked to me about getting my own life in alignment and harmony with the Bible.

"She was the one who had me make out lists of the good things I'd done, that was about half a page, and all the bad things, that amounted to 10 or 12 pages. She was off on that part, but the Bible as the Word of God, she really pushed that one. And I'd never heard that in all my years of school — not believing it anyway.

"I wrote a pamphlet about it then. The last night of her stay, she and I went into the church and knelt at the pulpit chairs. I remember I asked God for forgiveness, understanding and love, and I said if He really wanted me to serve Him, He would have to do something about it for I was at the end of my rope.

"Nothing cataclysmic happened then, except that I felt better mentally because I had been making so many negative confessions, and that prayer was the first positive one. It just washed out a lot of mental debris.

"Then Rosalind left. It was the fall of the year. Kids were back in school already. It must have been September. I was sitting in my office, an old dentist's office just around the corner from the church where I served — I'll show you that too when we get there. I bet you it's still there, though I haven't been back here since I left.

"I was praying. And I told Father outright that He could have the whole thing, unless there were real genuine answers that I wouldn't ever have to back up on.

"And that's when He spoke to me audibly, just like I'm talking to you now. He said He would teach me the Word as it had not been known since the first century if I would teach it to others.

"Well, I nearly flew off my chair. I couldn't believe that God would talk to me." He shakes his head slowly smiling. "It's just too fantastic. People won't believe it. But He spoke to me just as plainly as I'm talking now to you.

"But really, why is it so strange? When you think about it, you see in the Bible that all through the ages God talked to people. God talked to Moses, to all the prophets. God talked to Paul. All through the centuries, God has talked to people in times of great need. And that's what we have today — a terrific need. People are just so far from hearing and believing the Word of God.

"You don't get it in the theological schools. The Word is buried, just like it was in the time of Jeremiah. Oh, they had their priests, their higher echelons, their temples, their rituals. It all looked so religious, you know. But the Word of God was buried. Oh, they were teaching the people something — they called it the Word of God maybe, but the Word was buried. God spoke directly to Jeremiah.

"The Word is buried today. If there's no one around to teach it, God has to teach it Himself. You see, I am a product of my times. God knew me before the foundations of the world, just like He knew you and everyone else. We were all in God's foreknowledge from the beginnings.

"God knew I would believe His Word. And every day I am more and more deeply convinced of this ministry which teaches people the accuracy and integrity of God's Word. Without this ministry the world would be in far greater spiritual darkness about His Word. There would be less light in the world. Where else but in this ministry do you find the Word of God so living and real? This is truly a time of terrific need." Doctor nods his head abruptly, as if to punctuate his urgency.

"Well, I couldn't believe that God talked to me right then. You see, God's right here. He always has been here. He is still here. And God is willing and able to reveal everything to anyone or everyone. But we are just unable to receive it. We don't believe it. It's like, you can't pour a gallon of water into a teacup. It's just not big enough to receive it, take it all in. You have to make the cup bigger first. You build up the container, and then you fill it little by little. He fills us a little bit at a time as we can take it. He knows how much we can take because God knows everything. God doesn't waste His revelation on people who cannot believe it.

"Paul had to be tremendously built up to believe — receive — the mystery that had been hidden since before the foundations of the world. John, too, had to be built up to receive the revelation set forth in the book of Revelation. It's taken many years and a lot of trips and searching to build my believing to this point also. But God knows our hearts.

"Well, on the day God spoke to me, I couldn't believe it. But then I came to the point by the next day where I said to myself — maybe it's true. So the next day I talked to God again. I said, 'Lord, if it's really true what you said to me yesterday, if that was really you talking to me, you've got to give me a sign so that I really know, so that I can believe.'

"The sky was crystal blue and clear. Not a cloud in sight. It was a beautiful early autumn day. I said, 'If that was really you, and you meant what you said, give me a sign. Let me see it snow.' My eyes were tightly shut as I prayed. And then I opened them.

"The sky was so white and thick with snow, I couldn't see the tanks at the filling station on the corner not 75 feet away." Doctor relates this phenomenon in a joyous voice. The car swerves off the highway, onto a narrow black-top road, and the sign with the arrow reads: "Payne, 2 miles." The overcast sky turns restlessly over our heads, and the sparse sprinkling of snowflakes thickens on the windshield. Doctor laughs aloud.

"It reminds me of that day in 1942. It reminds me of that other time it snowed." We pull into a sleepy, small midwestern town. Around two corners, we're by a one-story building, the front of which is a many-paned display window.

"That's the old dentist's office that was my office," Doctor remarks. By now, the snow is swirling around us. At the corner stands the Marathon Gas Station. Doctor shakes his head from side to side. His face breaks into a ready smile. His eyes are blue, laughing or crying. "It reminds me of the day ...." he trails off. "That's where I was sitting when I prayed to God to teach me the Word and show me how. And when I opened my eyes, it was snowing so hard I couldn't see those gas pumps right there." He points to the pumps a dozen yards or more from the window. A car has just pulled in. The dentist's office is deserted now, empty through the window.

Doctor Wierwille steps on the gas, and our car cruises around the corner, pulling up beside a white wooden church, charming, quaint. Right beside it is the neat, rectangular parsonage.

"When we first got here, there was no parsonage. We lived for nearly a year as guests in four or five places. We moved around, Dotsie and Donnie and I, and then we finally got together the money to build a parsonage. It was during the war. Everything was very expensive. Materials were hard to find. Looks so small to me now, but when we moved in, we thought it was the greatest house in the world. Come on, let's see if anyone is home."

We climb out through the snow flurry making our way to the parsonage. An elderly lady with silver hair opens the door. Doctor explains who he is, that he built this house nearly thirty years ago. Handing her his card, he asks if we might come in and look around for a minute.

The lady is obliging. Hospitably she invites us in with a quick gesture, and the two fall into conversation about mutual acquaintances in former days in Payne. I look about the living room, dining room, kitchen. The construction is solid — dark, heavy woodwork surrounds beautiful wooden doors. Everything has the marks of careful and excellent workmanship. The layout is extremely simple and the use of space economical. I see the principles here that I have noted on the farm — a care for simplicity and functional beauty.

"And the Reverend ... of the ... Church, is he still here?" I overhear Doctor asking with genuine interest. I cannot hear her answer. Then Doctor goes on.

"Is he divorced yet?"

A look of extreme shock and discomfort passes over the lady's face.

"Divorced? Oh, my no," she insists. "You must be thinking of someone else. I don't know who you could be thinking about."

"And his wife? Is she still teaching up in Wisconsin?"

"Oh, yes," the silver-haired lady acknowledges reluctantly. "She has her Ph.D. you know, and she has been teaching up there the last three years. She has the youngest son with her. He must be in his twenties by now."

"So then they're separated, but not divorced," Doctor asks for clarification.

"Oh, no, no. They aren't separated, or divorced," she insists stubbornly. "Oh, no, they're very happily married."

"But she's been in Wisconsin these last three years. And is he still pastor here?" Doctor is regarding her with great compassion.

"Well, he has been in the hospital for several months now. He had one thing wrong and then another," the lady offers knowledgeably.

"And his wife, does she visit him often from Wisconsin?"

"No, no, she rarely comes here," the lady keeps up the conversation. "She's really busy up there, having a Ph.D. and all. She's extremely well-educated." The silver-haired lady covers, changing the direction of the emphasis.

"Well, thank you very much for letting us look at the house, Mrs. ..." Doctor addresses her graciously, shaking her hand, and we both walk out into the blowing snowflakes toward the church.

I am struck by their little conversation. The man is obviously ill, and his wife is not with him, and yet the woman would not admit to that, refused to see it. What difference did it make to her after all? Truth is truth. The Word is buried today, Doctor had said. When the Word is buried, there is no truth. She spoke what she knew, but it was not the truth, and Doctor gave her a chance to get honest more than once, to call a thing by its right name. He looked at her and loved her and stood on the truth. He did not give her more than she was able to receive.

"That's what the denominations do for a man," Doctor breaks into my reflections. "That's where I'd be today if I had not stood on the Word of God. Denominations don't care about teaching God's Word. They perpetuate themselves. They put people in straight-jackets, atrophy their lives. That's what Jesus meant when he asked the Pharisees: Why do you teach for doctrine the commandments of men?" Doctor's face is moved.

We walk up a flight of steps to the church door.

"Well, let's just see if this is open. We may have to get a key. The door should be locked on a weekday afternoon like this." On the side a sign reads: "The Church with the Open Door and the Open Bible, Evangelical Reformed Church." Doctor reaches out, turns the handle, and the door opens. We walk into the smell of fresh, sweet pine. The pews are of blonde wood, clean and neat. Two large stained-glass windows decorate two of the walls. On one wall, the one you see looking back from the pulpit, is a large representation of Jesus the Shepherd, holding a lamb in His arms, two more at His feet. Behind Him in the distance grazes a flock of tiny white sheep. "The Lord is my shepherd. I shall not want." He is a man in white flowing robes, girded about with a cloak of the deepest, richest ruby red. The whole picture breathes a transluscent tranquility.

To the right of the pulpit, slightly recessed, the other window of a serene and gentle blue is edged by a design of white lilies and green leaves. In the middle, small in a large blue sky, flies a white dove, a leaf in her beak — the Holy Spirit.

"You see, that holy spirit has been with me from the beginning, too," Doctor remarks distantly, surveying the empty church. "If this building is ever torn down, I shall buy those two windows. They are really beautiful, put together with love."

It doesn't take us long to look over an empty church. The Church is the called out of God. An empty building is an empty building, after all. We make our way down into the basement which is set up for Sunday school, little chairs perched under a couple of little tables.

"It's dead here. No life. No great power of God.

"This kitchen is where the elders gave it to me for preaching on tithing. They were hotter than fire crackers under the collar. They said, 'We told you — No money!' Then I had to make a stand. I said, 'You told me not to mention money, and I didn't mention it once. I mentioned only tithing. Now, you mind your business, and I'll mind mine which is to take care of this church like I think God wants me to take care of it.' That was it. After that, they didn't bother me anymore, and we had so much money come in, it even blew their minds."

Doctor seems relieved to see it all again. "I guess we've seen it, haven't we? This church isn't so hard for me to see. I wasn't here that long. It brings back memories, but I didn't have time to get so attached here. Let's go. I'll show you my other church in Van Wert. I really poured my heart and soul into it while I was there." He slips his card under a corner of the window sill near the guest book.

"Think they'll find it here sometime?" he asks jovially, and then walking out the door he starts on a new theme as I keep up behind him. "This is where I wrote my first book, too, *Victory in Christ.* You can see it in the display case at the Biblical Research Center. But I won't take it out for you. You see, I set down what I knew then, but I've learned lots more since. I didn't have the accuracy of the Word that I have now, after working it all these years, day after day. But that happened later."

We walk to the car, attacked on all sides by the threatening snowflakes.

"What happened to Rosalind Rinker?" I ask him, my thoughts still lingering on this woman who had such a strong influence on Doctor's memory from his years in Payne.

"Oh, she's still around. But she won't have much to do with me now — because our positions on the Holy Spirit differ. She can't accept that. But in those days, she really shook me up. She brought me back to the Bible. I had been brought up with that Word of God, with people around me operating the principles, but they couldn't teach them to me, and I had forgotten them in all my years of training at seminaries. She jarred me, at a time when I was searching and discouraged, with the idea again that the Word of God really was the Will of God. It got me started on the track."

Doctor starts the car and turns onto the road out of town.

"Well, that's Payne. You've seen it." Doctor pauses thoughtfully. "On October 2, 1942, right after that snowfall, we opened a radio broadcast called the Chimes Hour Youth Caravan on WLOK in Lima. That broadcast and the Sunday morning service made me, *made me,* go to the Word for two or three new teachings a week. It got me into the Word, got me growing in it, and kept me fluid.

"Ask Rhoda about the radio programs. We had them for years, changed the name of the program a few times. It was a good program. But the importance to me at that time was that it got me back to digging the Word.

"Between Rosalind Rinker and revelation, I had a lot of offers in Payne, from A.B. Dick Company, from Detroit, Michigan, as well as others. And I also got an offer from a church in Van Wert with an active membership of approximately 21 members. I took it.

"Lots of things got started in Payne — Karen Ruth was born in 1942. We moved to Van Wert to the parsonage in the summer of 1944 and right after that Mary was born.

"When I began teaching in Van Wert, Dr. Bassler of New Bremen, president of our Synod, was very disappointed. He said, 'I guess if you go to that church, we can·bury it a year later.' But we were there for fourteen years. It never did die until after I left, when the denomination saw to it that it died.

"We were in Van Wert only a few months when Dotsie got sick. Real sick. You ask her to tell you about it sometime. She got an attack of rheumatic fever, so bad the doctors were saying she'd never walk again, and the neighbors were saying she'd never pull through. It lasted a whole winter, but by spring, by the grace of God she was out of it.

"I didn't know the things I know now from the Word of God — but I was working it. That's when I began to get interested in the healing ministries such as Glenn Clark's camps featuring health through prayer in Minnesota. There were others: E. Stanley Jones, Rufus Mosley, Albert Cliffe, John Gaynor Banks. I had a tremendous hunger to know more. I invited people to come to Van Wert and teach my "Spiritual 40 Club." And I would listen to them and learn.

"But one of the finest educators I ever knew was a man named Lininger. Ever heard of him?" Doctor glances over at me and I shake my head. "I'm not surprised. But of all the people I heard, he was the finest educator. I met him when I got into the ministry in 1941, and he invited me to teach homiletics and get my Doctor's Degree at his school when I was ready.

"You've seen that degree on my office wall. It's from Pikes Peak Bible Seminary. You've never heard of that place either. Well, many seminaries don't recognize it, so they don't count my Doctor's Degree.

"The school isn't recognized, and yet Lininger had been the head of the Department of Education for the state of Colorado. He had studied in all the right schools and had gotten all the right degrees himself. But the established religious world just didn't go for his theories.

"You see, he said: 'If I can't teach what I know on a certain subject in three months, then I'm a lousy teacher.' He believed that the greatest education came from books. He and two or three other men got together and set up this program.

"They taught the principles of conveying material effectively. They were terrific and I learned a tremendous amount. These were top-notch men able to teach and communicate in a short amount of time. Many universities and colleges in the U.S. use Dr. Lininger's patterns now. And I use today, in my teaching, principles that I learned from him about teaching.

"But my Th.D. is not recognized in some theological circles. As far as they are concerned, I never received it. I went there a couple of summers after the war, finishing in 1948. There were many men that I learned from in those years.

"God sure must love us or we'd really be in the soup. It says in the Word that whoever hungers and thirsts ... shall be filled. If no one is around to teach you the Word, and you are hungry, then God has to teach you in the framework of your knowledgeable experience. For example, if you're an athlete, He'll do it through athletics. If you're a farmer, He'll teach you through farming.

"It was during those years in Van Wert that I really began to get into the depths of the Word of God. God taught me through people. He just showed me things, and my believing and discipline grew.

"Now looking back over my life, those years were like a dream. I don't think I could ever do it again. Every victory costs something. It cost me fourteen years from 8:30 a.m. to 2:30 a.m. I became an exile, estranged. I got out of circulation.

"Everybody wants to be loved and respected. Everybody wants to please. But the Word became the most exciting, the most thrilling thing in my life to me. It was like a toy to a child. I got excited over every iota of truth, every fragment. I just thrilled and thrill still at its inherent accuracy, its dynamic reality, its living truth. In those years of working the Word, it became my food, my life, my very breath." Doctor's voice rings with great love and conviction.

"Now I don't think I'd have the strength to do it again. Fourteen years, day after day, working the Word till it fit.

You get out of touch. The Word of God became everything to me, and people just thought I was kind of nuts.

"But why not? Why not get excited over God and His Word? Basically in the world today and all through history, there have been two roads to go — either the Stoic or the Epicurean — either the suicide trip or the live-it-up-till-death trip. And they both end up the same — killing yourself, destruction, although they look different to the eye — the fat trip and the skinny, deprived trip. They're basically the same end.

"But God offers us the wonderful middle way — the more abundant life. God's trip has the best of everything. The best. And few know about it because they don't know God's Word. How can you know it if you don't go to God's Word believing? That's what I'm here to teach people, that Word of God, so they can claim the more abundant life God offers us.

"What kept me going those years, day after day? I guess my drive came from really wanting to help people. Nowhere else can you get that peace, that joy, that contentment on the inside no matter what's happening around you. Nowhere, but in the Word of God.

"You see, God knew I'd believe to hear. I'm just as convinced of my ministry today as the Apostle Paul was. I have no doubts. I see that Word live in the heart and life of a man or a woman. I see it set them free, bring them peace and joy and fulfillment for the first time in their lives. I see it working. God's Word is perfect and it works.

"But those years in Van Wert, I was just beginning to put things together, little by little, beginning to see the greatness of it. Oh, honey, I just can't put it into words.

"There were people around and events. God brought people to me, and led me places and showed me things in those years in Van Wert. It was an exciting time, a learning time. God just kept leading me and encouraging me.

"I remember a woman in my congregation in Van Wert. Her name was Florence Scheidt. She was deaf. She couldn't hear a word. But she could understand whatever I preached on Sunday mornings. She always came to church, always sat in the exact same seat, the second row, second seat in from the aisle on the left. No matter how crowded it was, that was her seat.

"She was one of the most brilliant women I've ever met. She wore a hat that was fifty years old and a coat that was forty years old or something, but she was brilliant. She used to go to the library and read all the time when she wasn't working. She worked, sewing in an overalls factory in town. She would read about Church history, every detail, and then she taught me. She taught me tremendous love for Sunday School work, and for teaching the Word to young people.

"When I first came to Van Wert, people told me I'd never get along with her. No one else could, so they were sure I couldn't. But I did. We understood each other. She lived alone in a house full of cats, with newspapers all over the floor. I used to go over there to visit her sometimes, talk with her, and she supported me in the church.

"She was something else." Doctor laughs. "You know, the boss in the factory told her she was fired. Well, she had worked there for years, I don't know how long. She didn't hear them. She came right back to work the very next day. She said, 'You didn't hire me; you can't fire me,' and she went right back to work and worked till the day she died practically.

"She was burned in a fire in 1960. It happened when I was in England. I thank God I wasn't there. It tore my heart out when I heard about it. She'd been healed a few years before her death, of cancer, I think. I don't remember exactly. But she'd been completely delivered. She was my first major healing miracle.

"My father was a big help in those years too. He stepped in. He encouraged me. And my brother, Harry. He took an interest." Doctor pauses, staying his mind on those days.

"There was another person from our congregation in Van Wert. I was working the Word, putting it together, and he taught me a lot. I knew there was so much to the Holy Spirit field, but I was just beginning to see it.

"His name was Amil Schaffner. He was my hunting buddy and the man who taught me great love, prayer and humility. He'd rather dig ditches than do anything else in the world. From the sense-knowledge point of view, he lived in a ramshackle house. He dug ditches, dug septic tanks, did all kinds of jobs no one else wanted to do.

"He was married. In his sixties, I guess. His wife wore the strongest perfume you ever stumbled into. You could smell her coming to church before she even got to the door, when there was a north wind. Yep, that was old Amil.

"Thirty years before I met him, he had spoken in tongues. It happened on two occasions in his life. Once when he was a boy of eighteen years. The second time, the night his grandfather died. He always slept with his grandpa, and his grandpa always knelt next to the bed and prayed for a half hour or an hour before he went to sleep.

"On one such occasion when his grandpa was praying, Amil started to speak words he didn't understand. He told grandpa, and grandpa said he should ask God to forgive him, that he was sinning, that he shouldn't do it again.

"Well, he didn't until the night his grandfather died. He spoke strange words. But he felt tremendously guilty and asked God to forgive him again. Then he put that strange language out of his life.

"He shared these things with me over a period of time. But I was working the Word in the Holy Spirit field at the time. Certain events happened in my life leading me to receive the holy spirit. And the night I led him into receiving the holy spirit he just cried like a baby. He cried, 'My God, why? Why do I have to come to this knowledge of the truth at the very end of my life, when I could have enjoyed it all along since I was a boy?'

"He was something. He taught me a lot. He always wore old bib overalls, a jacket and big rubber boots. And he was always dirty. One particular summer, we'd been talking for months about digging out a basement — our church was very small. We needed more room, and everybody talked — the elders, the church fathers, the congregation, but no one could agree. Nothing happened, just a lot of talk.

"But old Amil, he put his believing to work. One morning very early, right at sunrise, he showed up with his team of horses and a scoop, and he just started digging it out. He did it. Everybody else just talked.

"That was in 1949, I guess. Rhoda had already come to work for me. Up until that basement was dug out, we had no central heating in the church, just two old pot-bellied stoves. We used to start them up early Saturday night in the winter, and then everyone would warm up with singing on Sunday morning. My congregation in Van Wert used to really boom it out. When you get with groups, there's just nothing like singing together to get everyone turned on and keyed to really listen. We'd really warm up the old church."

Doctor shifts in his seat, chuckling, and then a silence falls over him. I have hardly been noticing the countryside for listening in absorbed attention. But now suddenly, I realize that the snow has stopped. Not enough fell even to cover the ground. The branches of stark, black trees are waving wildly. A wind has risen, chasing the clouds away, and a miraculous patch of clear, blue sky emerges ahead of us.

I begin asking Doctor questions, "But what was the event that happened before you led Amil Schaffner into receiving the holy spirit? What happened?"

"I guess that day was the second most important event in my life — after the day that God spoke to me in that old dentist's office in Payne — the day I received into manifestation the holy spirit and spoke in tongues. I had been searching for years for more understanding of the Word, of the power we have in Christ Jesus. I'd tried all kinds of denominations, all kinds of trips. I'd gone to Pentecostal groups, to all kinds. I can't remember them all.

"I had worked all 385 verses in the Bible that spoke of the Holy Spirit. I knew every verse from memory. I had seen in the book of Acts how they spoke in tongues, and I'd gone to every group I'd heard of that I thought might give me more light on it.

"I'd seen them rolling in the aisles, you know. I'd seen them lying on the floor, jumping up and down, running, crawling on their hands and knees to catch the Holy Spirit, throwing books to hit the Holy Spirit. Oh, I don't know what else. I saw everything.

"I'd asked the greatest minds, theologians, in the country about receiving the holy spirit. No one could help me. I just knew that all I was seeing was flesh, not spirit.

"I had tremendous natural fear of doing anything that would make me look foolish. Yet everyone of those groups was doing something really foolish. I was afraid I'd do something terrible if I received.

"But I hungered to receive the fullness of it. I wanted to speak in tongues. I could see in the book of Acts the power of the Spirit moving Peter from a scared man behind locked doors to addressing the multitudes of Jerusalem boldly and fearlessly on the day of Pentecost.

"Rufus Mosley prayed for me in Van Wert. He had laid hands on me. Nothing happened. The second time Rufus Mosley visited me, he said, 'Whenever you receive the fullness of the holy spirit, you will really be able to help others receive because you have quested; you have understanding.' But he was at a loss to help me receive. Rufus said, 'I'm full, but I can't give it to you, and I don't know why.'

"The day after Rufus Mosley said those words to me, a piece of mail came regarding a Full Gospel Rally in Tulsa, Oklahoma. Oh, all the great names were going to be there, including a would-be-rising star in Pentecostalism — Oral Roberts.

"By then, I'd had it. I wasn't even going to go. I don't know what made me change my mind exactly. But I said to Father, I'd go, but it would be the last time; and if I did not receive, I'd leave. I said: there must be something wrong. I was sick and tired of looking, but I made up my mind I'd go this one last time.

"That was the winter of 1951. I flew to Tulsa, checked into the hotel, and went over to where the meeting was that night. It was a big rally. I met someone, told him my need, and he got all excited. He said he'd introduce me to some great men. They'd lay hands on me and lead me into tongues.

"So before the meeting they got together, nine great men, in one room. They started praying, then three or four laid hands on me, and finally one of them said, 'Speak another language.' So I spoke in Greek. I quoted the first chapter of John. Well, they started jumping up and down. They thought it was great. They didn't know Greek. They said I had received and told me to speak in another language.

"So I did. I spoke in Hebrew — quoted from Genesis, and they just got all excited, congratulating themselves about it.

"But in my heart, I knew I wasn't speaking in tongues. You see, they'd just told me to speak in another language; they never taught me or showed me the accuracy of the Word on this. They said 'another language' and I spoke another language.

"At the big meeting that night one of the men stood up and told the two or three thousand that they had just led an Evangelical and Reformed minister from Van Wert into tongues. He was on an ego trip about it, but I was just sick of the whole thing. Sick of lying. I knew it was a lie. I was ready to go home.

"So I left the meeting, slipped out, went to my hotel and called the airport. I was all set to check out. But a funny thing had happened — there was a blizzard in Tulsa. All the planes were grounded. So I couldn't get a plane. I tried the trains — they were all snowed in. The buses — same thing. The city was snowbound. I just couldn't get out!

"Well, I called back the airport, and they said they could put me on standby for the night. I asked the girl on the phone, 'Does this happen all the time?' She said, 'No, this is the first time.'" Doctor punctuates his story with a rumbling laugh. He continues his account, pointing the car squarely towards the widening patch of blue sky.

"The next morning, I still hadn't left town. I went to breakfast at the hotel, sat down next to a straight guy. He looked me over and recognized me. He began, 'Aren't you that Evangelical and Reformed preacher who spoke in tongues last night?' I said, 'Yes, but it was a damn lie.' Then he said he knew I was damned because I cussed. That ended our conversation.

"Then a woman came over to me, and said, 'I think God sent a man here to meet your need. Meet me at 9 a.m.' I thought, 'Women never tell the truth.' But then I reconsidered, since I was stuck in town anyway. So I decided to meet her.

"I got to the place she said at 9 a.m. and there she was. She introduced me to a man named J. E. Stiles. He'd come in from the West Coast. A few days before, God had told him to go to Tulsa to minister the holy spirit to one man. We talked for a few minutes, and he suggested we go into the rally to hear Oral Roberts and then meet for lunch.

"So that's what we did. At lunchtime Stiles came in with his wife and the pianist. I just remember thinking to myself, 'There aren't going to be any women around when I get the holy spirit.' I was just watching and waiting. Lunch was kind of light talk — we talked about Oral Roberts, the Holy Spirit, lots of stuff. When we were done, I picked up the check, and then Stiles turned to his wife and said, 'Honey, I'm going with VP.' She said something to him like, 'How long will you be?' And he said, 'That's none of your business.' That was it, and my opinion of him as a man went up 99 percent. His stature increased in my eyes, just from the way he handled her.

"We left the women and went up to my room. Stiles began to teach me from Acts 2:1-4, and many other verses. Also Luke 11:11, where it talks about fathers giving gifts to their children: If a child asked for bread, would the earthly father give him a stone? He just went over and over those things, used those verses in Luke hundreds of times to get that fear out of me. He just drove it home to me — God wouldn't give a lousy gift.

"We worked till 3 p.m. Finally, I believed and spoke in tongues. I didn't know the language. It was like a burning light. It just cooked me on the inside. Such a flood came out.

"For the next half hour, Stiles had me speak and stop, just start and stop. Then he left. But I went on all night — speaking in tongues, praying in my understanding, reading from the Word. I was up all night, higher than a kite. I never ate. I couldn't sleep. I was so thrilled, so overjoyed and burning.

"And that has been the greatest night of my life. Father showed me things that night. Some of them have come to pass, and others not yet.

"The next day, I don't remember much what happened. I was so high on spirit. My senses just didn't seem to make much sense, but so what? The thing I remember is that I dropped in at the meetings and someone was making an appeal for Jack Coe's Orphanage. I had a twenty-dollar bill in my wallet, and I just threw it in. The first piece of mail I opened when I got home was a check for forty dollars. The Lord just doubled my money back to me. And since then it's been miracle after miracle.

"You see, learning is a process. You don't learn overnight. The holy spirit field — that's the field God raised me up for. There's not a question that cannot be answered biblically. And there's no one I can't lead into speaking in tongues if they are Christian and want to do it.

"No matter how much knowledge you have of God, God seldom allows you to teach more than people are able to receive. Some things God taught me that night in Tulsa, I've never taught — no one would have been able to receive them."

Doctor Wierwille swings the car down a long tree-lined street. We're in a town larger than Payne. I have hardly been noticing the road. I turn to him with a questioning glance.

"This is Van Wert, honey," Doctor is saying, his voice soft and mellow. He sighs barely audibly. "Brings back a lot of memories.

"There's L. G. Purmort Insurance Company that insured some things at the 18th World's Fair in Chicago, the one that burned down. And over there, Alspach Funeral Home, you see that? Both of his sons were with me in the ministry. One son was killed. He stepped on a high tension wire. Both of them were with me on the Youth Caravan radio program. And over there is where Mohler was the minister. He went to Washington later as a Representative. And there, you see, the Van Wert Gospel Gift Shop? We started it — that's where we had our Print Shop. Then when we left for our world teaching tour, we sold it to the Schaadts. And there's the school where my first three kids went."

Doctor drives slowly through the streets, around corners, pointing out one thing after another to me. He rounds another corner, pulling up by a neat red brick church. Next to it stands the white wooden parsonage. We get out of the car and walk around.

"Over there behind the house was the dog kennel where we kept the dogs. I've always loved dogs — good hunting dogs. And over in that lot, we had some ponies." He waves his hand at a grassy block.

"We used to graze them over there, and one day the mayor called me because one of the ponies was foaling. He was irate. He said it was a shame, that I should run over and cover her with a blanket or something because it was too embarrassing to see what was going on. Yep, that's how it was."

We walk along the sidewalk to the church door. I wonder if this one will be open too, even though it is a weekday afternoon.

"It's been changed around, the entrance. It used to be at the back and now they've moved it to the side. Let's go in. The Lord had the last one open for us." He reaches for the handle and turns it. The church is unlocked. We walk into a darkened bare interior. The pews are light brown wood. No stained glass colors the walls. The atmosphere is numb and lifeless. Doctor turns to me with a heavy sigh.

"This is the first time I've been back," he begins slowly. "I'd never have come back but to show you. It's so hard on my heart. So many years I spent here, so many memories, so much time working with these people, so much happened here. Back here was my office and across from it, Rhoda's office. They've torn them both out now, changed everything.

"Do you know why these 'Reserved' signs are on the last five rows on both sides? Because so few people come now on Sundays, they have to get them to sit up front somehow, so it won't look too empty. That's how they do it.

"When I got here in 1944, the congregation was approximately 21 people, but it grew fast. We filled her up on Sundays. When I left in 1957, I left a full house behind. Over there, that's where Florence Scheidt used to sit. Bless her heart. I can almost see her there now."

I follow Doctor down the back steps into the basement.

"This is what old Amil dug out for us. We elevated the whole building. And that clock on the wall — that's our old clock from the radio programs. We'd send the program out right from this church."

The basement is large and square. Again I notice the craftsmanship — the solidity, simplicity and usefulness. One wall is a large mural of Jesus and the children. They stand around a monumental but gentle Jesus, all colors and costumes. The picture evokes a touching mood.

"I should have had it painted on canvas so that we could have taken it with us, not on the wall like that. It sure is a beautiful picture. He really captured something there. Oh well," Doctor shrugs in acceptance.

"Back there is the kitchen — I remember tiling that thing. When I came back from Tulsa, Mal George and his wife, Jan, were the first ones I led into receiving the holy spirit. They live in New Knoxville now, both of them teachers, have seven kids. They stood with the ministry over twenty years now, never wavered.

"We tiled this kitchen floor together. After Amil dug it out, and things were built in. I remember it was on a New Year's Eve — we always had a party. Everyone had gone home about one o'clock, but the four of us were sitting here still, high, just nobody sleepy. So we said, 'Let's tile the floor.' It was cold in here. It was winter and the heating wasn't in here yet. So we turned on the oven, and my Dotsie and Jan would slip those linoleum tiles in to warm them up, and we tiled the whole floor that night. I don't know when we got done. But we sure had a good time doing it. That's the very floor."

Doctor strolls through the room, his hands in his raincoat pockets. The walls are of paneled pine boards and folding doors are available to break the space up into smaller sections. It reminds me of the basement of the Biblical Research Center.

"But how did you get the class started?" I ask him. "It was happening while you were here in Van Wert."

"A lot of things happened here in Van Wert," Doctor remarks distantly.

"After that trip to Tulsa lots of things fell into place. God just keeps giving it to you as you can take it. Someone in Tulsa gave me the name of B. G. Leonard, or sent my name to him, I can't remember which. Anyway, after Tulsa I began to get his monthly newsletter from Calgary, Alberta, Canada.

"I never read that thing. It was so badly printed, you could hardly make out a word. I never read it for two years. And then a couple of years after Tulsa, I had been working the Word about laying on of hands. I'd worked every scripture and seen how they worked together perfectly.

"That particular day, just after I'd worked it through, I'd gotten B. G. Leonard's newssheet. Well, I just crumpled it up and threw it in the wastebasket as usual. I did some other things, and later that day I took the wastebasket out to burn the rubbish. As I shook it out, this thing which was on the bottom, fell out on top of the heap in the incinerator — opened.

"There staring me in the face was an article about laying on of hands. I read the first two lines fast, and they were perfectly accurate. So I pulled the whole thing out of the fire before it burned and read it through. The whole article was exactly what I had come up with in my months of research. So I went in and called B. G. Leonard on the telephone.

"He told me he loved me, but I couldn't come up to see him because he was in the middle of a class. So I took the next plane to Calgary. His place was called the Christian Training Centre.

"B. G.'s place was a real dive. There was a Jewish store on the first floor, B. G.'s work place was on the second, and his living quarters on the third. I walked in and he was halfway through his announcements. They must have lasted an hour and a half. Then when he was through, he took out his violin and played for a while.

"And then he started preaching. Boy, oh, boy, was he with it! He taught his heart out for another hour and a half. Then everyone left, and I just sat there. He said, 'Hi, ya, there, Wierwille, I thought I told you, you couldn't come.' And I said, 'Yeh, but I didn't hear you.' 'Well, where are you staying?' he asked me, and I told him. And he said, 'Why, you're in the middle of the red light district. That's all whores!'

"Then he got me settled in another place. I spent quite a time with him. He was fearless. He'd been raised a Roman Catholic, been a cowboy, worked in an insane asylum. He'd been through a lot. But he loved me, and I knew it. You see, the denominations were beginning to dislike me because I smoked or I didn't smoke enough. But B. G. didn't care what you looked like; he just wanted to know what you had on the inside.

"He loved me, and I learned some stuff from him. He had tremendous believing. That's why I love the guy. A man with a ministry from God, if he stands for one day or one year, he's blessed the world for a lifetime. If he cops out the second day, God doesn't like that; but if he stands for one day, it's worth a lifetime.

"The summer of 1953, our whole family went up — Dotsie and Donnie and some of the others from Van Wert. We took his whole trip — really learned a lot about the other manifestations of the holy spirit. But he worked from personal experiences. I worked what he taught from the accuracy of the Scriptures. When I came home, I made up my mind that I was going to tie the whole thing together from Genesis to Revelation. So I did, and in October, I had the very first 'Power for Abundant Living' Class.

"At that time, the Foundational Class and the Advanced Class were together — the whole thing in two weeks. But the syllabus today is basically the same. The basic principles from the Word are the same. The class has filled out. But I knew the greatness of our age — the age of holy spirit and that every truth must fit in the framework of the manifestations. I just had to teach it to somebody.

"I taught without a syllabus, but the class was the same. You could throw the syllabus away now and I could still teach it. It's a burning reality in my soul.

"Today I'm concerned with finding greater keys to make the reality of operating all the manifestations clearer, simpler. I've just been over ten or twelve records in the Word of God that I know. I look at the whole picture to see how I can do a better job than I ever did before.

"Really, it's looking at techniques of presenting biblical truth. You know the record in Samuel when he was a boy and God called him? Samuel thought Eli was calling him. Eli had to teach him that it was God calling, and to answer and ask what God wanted. You see, without someone's teaching us, we can't learn about the manifestations. Unless someone teaches us, we'll always be in confusion. We must learn that the things of the Lord can be taught just as well as the things of the secular world.

"The Word has all the keys in it — all the keys to writing and presenting and teaching the Word of God. Research is not only knowledge, but the communication thereof. What good would it do for me to know if I couldn't share it to the degree of your understanding?

"Every class I teach live, I teach according to the needs of the people I'm teaching. But the tape and film classes are taught according to the accuracy of God's Word.

"Well, I guess I got away from Van Wert in the fifties," Doctor says cocking his head a little to one side and raising his eyebrows.

"Somewhere in there I wrote the first holy spirit book. I can't remember exactly what year. Ask Rhoda. She remembers those dates. (Rhoda said 1954.) I'd been working those 385 scriptures and they began to all fall into place. That's when I took a week off. I moved into the Marsh Hotel in town. Didn't tell anyone where I was. But I had to get off alone to put it all together. So the neighbors said I was getting a divorce! How do you like that one?

"I spent a week putting that whole thing together — the first edition. We printed the pages ourselves, then glued the covers together, bound it, and there we had it, eighty-seven massive pages, each book handmade. That was something. We're having the sixth edition printed now of that book: *Receiving the Holy Spirit Today*. It's a great piece of research.

"Lots of the stuff I teach is not original. Putting it all together so that it fit — that was the original work. I learned wherever I could, and then I worked that with the Scriptures. What was right on with the Scriptures, I kept; but what wasn't, I just dropped.

"Vale from Florida was the one who taught us about interpretation and prophecy. But he didn't understand the other manifestations. It took B. G. Leonard and others to teach us healing and believing.

"But in the holy spirit field, our piece of research is the most thorough and original coverage of the subject. And believe me, I've seen about everything in that field. No one really goes into it. There's so much confusion and wrong teaching, people don't come near it. But when you really open up the Word of God, it's so clear and simple. So that was the first edition of the holy spirit book, back then.

"Oh, I've added depth, a lot more sharpness and clarity to that original study in the later editions, but it was all there then." Doctor roams the walls with his eyes, recapturing something written there, that only he can see, that only he recalls.

"Do you know that three times in those early years people tried to kill me?" he remarks suddenly, facing me squarely. I wait, hoping for details, but Doctor relaxes his shoulders in a barely noticeable gesture, and then launches into a new theme.

"There was another person in Van Wert, who was very important to me while I was working the Word, fitting the parts together so that I could comprehend and share the knowledge. And that was Dr. E. E. Higgins. She was a lady osteopathic surgeon from Chicago. I met her there, and she was in the first class.

"She would call me every night between 2:30 and 4:30 a.m. She knew that if I was still up, I'd be there in my office at that time. And she'd ask me one question: 'What did God teach you from His Word today?' And I would tell her. That was my release. She had a great hunger for the Word, and teaching it to her would just crystalize it in my mind.

"God told me to teach the Word of God to others, but He never told me to how many people. She used to come to Van

Wert on weekends. She'd stay at the "Y." She'd say it was like coming home. She gave me my first copy of Bullinger's *How To Enjoy The Bible*. She said, when she first heard me teach, that I taught like he wrote, and I'd never met the man or even read his stuff.

"She used to invite me up to Chicago once a month or so. She'd rent a room and invite the people she had contact with, prominent business and professional men from the Chicago area. I'd come up and teach — forty or fifty people there.

"She taught me the great respect and love I have for the human body — the tenderness of it. She loved the body, like I love the Word of God. She just stood in awe of how magnificently it was put together. She rid me of my hang-ups, that false stuff, and taught me the beauty of the human body. We used to talk about the human body — where the life was located.

"And she would call every night those years and ask me what God had taught me today. She did me a tremendous favor. I would release what I had learned, so that the next day, I was open, thirsting, to receive more of the Word." Doctor comes to a halt, takes a final glance around the basement room, and starts walking towards the stairs.

"I could go on and on. It just all comes back to me. I haven't thought about this stuff for years, for decades. I could just talk and talk, but I couldn't tell it all to you. Have you seen enough? Come on, let's go." Without turning to look a last time, he steps out of the heavy door, allowing it to swing shut behind us.

"So much of my life I spent here. It's unbelievable." We walk quickly to the car. The wind has shifted. The clouds move majestically against a canopy of blue. The air is mellowed by a comforting warmth. I imagine the wind has turned from north to southwest. It carresses my face gently.

Doctor starts the car and we pull away from the curb. He never once looks back.

"We'll drive by the house on South Washington Street, the house we moved to after I resigned from the church in 1957," Doctor proposes in a tone like the dawning of a new day.

"Yes, but how is it you left? Why did you resign? What happened?" I feel that I've missed something.

"I resigned shortly after we got back from our missionary study tour to India. I'll tell you about that too." We drive a few minutes in silence. Then Doctor slows the car along a tree-lined street.

"There she is, the house we moved into," he points to a large old house, with a round-tower corner, "609 South

Washington. It's a beautiful house. We moved here as a temporary place to get started. We figured when the time came we'd move to a more permanent place.

"One lady offered us a 25-acre plot near Chicago. But I didn't take it. Also in Fort Myers, Florida, people offered me a place, the Junior Chamber of Commerce in Florida. I looked at other places; I had a vision of a headquarters for research work where I could reach a handful of people, for I wondered if more than fifty would ever respond to my ministry.

"Some people thought I should go to Troy, Ohio. They found us a big house, thinking it would be ideal. It had lots of acres and we already had work going in Troy and in Piqua. But that stuff all went on after we moved here to South Washington Street, during the four years that we lived there.

"I needed time to work the Word, I needed the freedom to teach the depths of what I knew. We thought this house was right till we found something permanent, so we just rented. It was big, all trimmed in oak, hardwood interiors. On the stairway landing there was a beautiful stained glass window with a loveseat. The capacity was fifty or so, but it wasn't long before it was overflowing when we met Sunday and Thursday nights. Some nights it was just the family, because we stuck together through thick and thin.

"When I resigned from the church in 1957, Sam Rolsten, the chairman of the Board of the Consistry, wanted me to stay on; but I needed that time and that freedom to work the Word. It wasn't from my congregation that pressure came.

They flocked to church every Sunday. People were tithing. My church was thriving. But, you see, the denomination became too confining. Too confining," Doctor repeats, swinging the car back into motion along South Washington Street and out of town.

"You were going to tell me about your trip to India, and how it came about," I remind him, wanting to hear the details. Doctor drives deliberately, concentrating, as though setting the events clearly in his mind before starting.

"In the fifties, I don't remember exactly what year, I made a trip to Honduras because the Evangelical and Reformed Church had mission work there and our church had been supporting it. We had raised money for it, and I wanted to see at first-hand what they were doing with it.

"One of the missionaries there was Bertha Scheidt, from our own church in Van Wert, and I arranged to visit and stay there for a few weeks. I was terribly shocked by what I saw on the mission field in Honduras. I simply couldn't believe it. At that time, I decided we'd go to other lands to take a look at mission work without being given hospitality by my denomination.

"What shocked me? The poverty of the country, the good life of the nationals who had salaamed the mission cause, the high-on-the-hog living of the missionaries, the favors extended to them by the U.S. banana company who in turn was paying their Honduras' employees fifty cents a day for 'slave labor.'

"Oh, they gave me the guided tour. I was their guest. I taught in churches there. But I had my belly full; I couldn't believe that mission work could be so enslaving. You see, they always spoke of all they had done for the people — hospitals, schools, all that trip — but that's all counterfeit. All the time the people were enslaved.

"In the fifties here in Van Wert, we had many visitors. One of them was Bishop K. C. Pillai, and he invited us to come to India in 1955. My first reason for going was that I wanted to see if people would respond more to the Word in the East than in the Occident. Bishop Pillai was a converted Hindu who opened up for us the Eastern customs behind many scriptures. He had taken the class and had been teaching Orientalisms to us here. He said that Hindus would believe and would want to hear the Word of God.

"We went as a family, Dotsie and I and the three oldest children. John Paul was two months old, so he stayed with his aunt, Dotsie's sister. It had never happened before that a man of God and his whole family went on a missionary tour. And I went unaffiliated, not under the flag of any denomination.

"We left in the fall of 1955, came back the spring of 1956. We went through Lebanon, Syria, Jordan, Israel, Egypt, and I constantly observed and considered the foreign mission programs on the spot.

"We ended up spending three months going all over India. I observed them all — the Roman Catholics, the Protestants, my own denomination, the Presbyterians, Methodists, Anglicans, the Salvation Army and the Pentecostal groups.

"The things I had seen in Honduras were magnified in India. They were basically 'Rice Christians' — you give them rice, and they are your Christians. The Word wasn't living anywhere in those groups.

"And the nationals? The non-Christians, they were fabulously responsive. I met with governors-of-states and other top men in the Central Government of India, as well as leading professionals and businessmen. I was the first minister invited to speak before the Jain convention.

"They responded because we brought with us only a teaching and research ministry of blessing to the people, irrespective of religious allegiance, with no acquisition of property and with no threat to the freedom of the nationals.

"The response of the denominations — my own included — was supremely non-loving, even vociferously opposed. The National Council of Churches in India informed me that I was not representing the Evangelical and Reformed Church, which I never claimed anyway. From then on I stopped all mission support except one dollar per year.

"When we returned to the U.S., I saw even more clearly how irresponsive people were to the Word. But it follows. You see, in the East people put God first, right or wrong. In the United States people put money first or power or pleasure. It's hard to find a place for God.

"I could see that America was at a very low ebb spiritually. We had a lot of religion, but we sure lacked knowledge of the accuracy and integrity of God's Word, so that Christianity was just a name, a flag, a title.

"I wrote a long study of my research and observations called *The Dilemma of Foreign Missions*. That caused some furor from the top echelons. But that has all passed. I just needed the freedom to work and teach to whoever was hungry. I didn't need the pressure, the man-made rules.

"That's when I resigned in 1957 and we moved to that house on South Washington Street. I asked twelve people to stand with me for one year. But many of them were not in the church. I was still hung up on the denomination. I told others to stay with that church. I didn't want to disrupt anything, cause division or hardship. I didn't want to hurt anyone, so I told them to stay with the denomination.

"Now if I had to do it again, I would do what Paul did — take all my people with me across the street, to the school of Tyrannus, or whatever, and teach the Word to anyone who wanted to hear. But at that time I didn't want to hurt anybody's feelings in my denomination, even though they cared little about hurting mine.

"There were people who stood with me: the Joneses, the Georges, the Permanns. I don't remember all their names right now. It was a stand. And all that time we were keeping our eyes opened for a place to make our permanent headquarters. Sara was born in 1957.

"One night Harry came in and said, 'If you want to have the headquarters at our old farm, I will remodel the house and pay for it, and we'll start the work there the best we can.'

"I called a Board of Directors meeting. The president wanted me to move to Troy, and he got turned off. I must have lost thirty people that day who thought I was totally wrong in my leading.

"We started the work at the farm in New Knoxville in 1959, and moved there in February of 1961. We opened the work in the basement of our house. That fall we had much more interest than I'd anticipated, so we began work on the Biblical Research Center. You know, that building is a National Home, a prefab built by Cleon White, one of the original elders from Payne, Ohio.

"There was no change — just a change in location. I never asked anyone to join me there. We just taught the Word, and whoever wanted could come and listen.

"I still miss the many hours of research. I miss it these weeks, but the ministry has so many segments. I have to do a thousand things. But you discipline your life to carry the whole ministry.

"That move to New Knoxville has been the finest move we ever made. It's a quiet, rural atmosphere. I love that place. I love to see the corn and beans grow. I love to see the wind playing across the wheat. I love the beauty of the place because people come and get blessed and I get blessed."

In my mind I flash a glimpse of the farm we left only a few hours ago, the grounds lighted with peace and love, and I am suddenly overjoyed that we are headed back, that we are going home.

"Well, we're on our way home," Doctor says suddenly, turning a smile in my direction. "What else do you want to know?"

I think a few seconds and begin asking questions.

"What happened then, after you moved to the farm? How did the ministry begin to grow? There is quite a difference, I saw from looking at the old Way magazines, between the ministry in 1965, say, and what was happening by 1970. That is only five years, but what were the events and people surrounding the big change?"

Doctor ponders the road in front of him as he drives. His brows are drawn together in concentration. It is as though he carefully formulates his train of thought before speaking.

"There have been many changes since we moved to the farm. The growth has been almost unbelievable. And everything at the right time, just as we were able to handle it and not a moment before.

"Most of the people I had taught were church-goers, in the old ritual syndrome. They would hear the Word, but then they'd go back to the same old church rituals. And I was gearing my teaching, my approach, to those people, not to the young, or to those outside of the church. I did that for fifteen years. It took me time to wise up.

"But God doesn't waste His efforts. I suppose those early years on the farm were a time of building the foundational structure for this entire ministry, solving problems while we were on a small, local scale. We learned a great deal. It was a chance to practice full-scale the principles of the Word, unconfined by other organizations. This entire ministry is built on the Word of God.

"The first class on the farm began on Easter Sunday, April, of the year we moved here. It met once or twice a week and ran all the way into July. We did it like that as an experiment. The second class that year was the Advanced Class later on that summer. In between those two classes, Bishop Pillai taught on Orientalisms. We had no Summer School here other than that.

"But in 1962, we began classes in Estrangelo Aramaic with Dr. Lamsa himself. He is the foremost scholar in Aramaic in the world even today. At that time, he was working on his own translation of the Old Testament which was later published. Several in that class had great ability — Bernita Jess who teaches our Aramaic classes now and Jim Chamberlin — those were two of them anyway.

"By that summer, we had already begun the original part of the Biblical Research Center which was completed and dedicated in December of 1961. And the day after Christmas,

I went to teach the first class in California. From there, I made a trip to Samoa to visit Dr. Pouesi. I had met him at B. G. Leonard's in Canada. He was a skilled surgeon and a minister, and he came from a royal background. He had been converted to Christianity and had joined Leonard's class to learn more. He invited me to Western Samoa and I went, taught for two weeks, and then came home. The climate was so hot and humid. Dr. Pouesi, Bishop Pillai, Dr. Lamsa — they were all people from those years. They came here, taught us what they knew, and we learned many things from them.

"And we had camps, summer camps. We had one in Wisconsin the summer of 1959 and in Indiana the summer of '60, Miamisburg, Ohio the summer of 1961.

"But in 1962, we had our first Summer School and camp on the farm, and every summer since then. It's a fantastic program. Renewed Mind is one of our classes. Where else in the world can someone go and hear teaching on how to renew your mind? Nowhere. That's why our camps and Summer School program are unique.

"You can't get such teaching anywhere else in the world. And we are geared to the whole family. We just surround a family with love and build them all up together in the Word. You see, the Christian family is God's basic unit. We show people how and help them live the more abundant life together as a family." Doctor breaks off suddenly, as though something new had just flashed through his mind.

"That first summer here — that was the summer of my son Donnie's motorcycle accident. It was a miraculous healing." Doctor shakes his head.

"Could you tell me more about it?" I almost break in, wanting to have more details. Doctor sighs, smiles at me with resignation, reliving a long life, but his smile is willing.

"Donnie had a bike which I fixed up for him while he was away at college. I always had a bug for a bike, ever since that first one from high school. He came home that summer for a visit and he took the bike for a spin. Another boy on his motorcycle went with him. They charged down Route 29 and were on their way back here, as I recall.

"Donnie told me about it later. We didn't actually see it happen. But apparently the other boy didn't have a windshield, and he was laying low for speed. Donnie was ahead of him. Donnie made a signal and slowed down to turn, but the other boy just didn't see him till it was too late. Donnie was thrown into the fence. The other boy rolled out of the way of his bike because Donnie had yelled at him to roll just in time. The other boy's bike went right up Donnie's back and over the top of his head.

"Well, the neighbors who witnessed the accident started gathering; someone called us and someone else got a doctor and even called an ambulance. By the time Dotsie and I got there, a doctor was already present. He told us that Donnie's back might be broken and he could have internal injuries. I don't know.

"When we got there Donnie asked us to minister to him. And Dotsie and I did. He believed. He has great believing, that boy. He asked us to take him home and we had to help him.

"We drove him home. There were a whole bunch of people at our house for a barbecue. As we drove up everyone was silent. Everyone praying, I guess. That was a Saturday when all this happened.

"Donnie lay on the floor downstairs. We fixed him a spot in the living room. We had to help him to the bathroom several times. But at about eleven, he told us all to go to bed, to leave him, and we did. We found out the next morning that during the night he had gotten up and gone to the bathroom by himself.

"I guess it was a terrific crisis for him. But that's what it comes down to — either it's God's Word or it isn't. You believe God, you act on it — you walk on it — and that's just what Donnie did.

"The next day was Sunday. And that morning Donnie asked to go to church in town. He realized people would judge the power of God through his actions. And his actions were positive. So we all went to church, all the men together. That sure blessed a lot of people — to see him up and walking around. But that's the power of God when you believe. He never had any pain, anything after that night, no limps, nothing. He just believed God, got delivered, and a whole lot of people were blessed. Well, you asked me about healing before, and I just remembered that one. We've had others in our own family. Ask Dotsie about Mary, about Sara. She'll tell you. I can't remember them, but Donnie's accident I just remembered." Doctor smiles again warmed by the memory of God's victory.

"How did you raise your children to have such tremendous believing?" I want to know.

"Honey, on the Word. The best we knew how, according to God's Word. Dotsie raised them. I was involved in my work, my ministry. I used to tell them they were the greatest kids in the whole world — and they were — but I never hesitated to correct them, to tell them where they were off, and how to get back on, or put them back on when they were small.

"It's been different with John Paul and Sara. You see, J.P. was born eleven years after Mary. It's almost like we had two families. I learned a lot in those years. By the time J. P. and Sara came along, we were really involved in so many things.

"I never had a great deal of time with the children, so whatever time I had, I lived it to the fullest with them. It was always short and sweet. I would take Donnie hunting or fishing for a day or half a day — teach him what I knew. Or we'd do something together as a family. We didn't have a whole lot of time together, but I made some, and they were always great.

"You see," Doctor breaks off and shifts in his seat, considering his words, "You see, God always comes first. That Word is life. I can't tell you exactly how we raised those kids or how I live with Dotsie, what our relationship is like. But the best way I could say it, for me and Dotsie, is it's an awareness of her presence. We don't spend all that much time together. We never had a lot of time. But there was always that awareness of her presence. In the Bible God made Eve for Adam as a help-meet, as a companion — not a baby-maker or a housekeeper.

"That's how it is at home. When Dotsie is around, I am aware of her presence. It's a comfort to me, a quiet joy, an understanding. And if she is not there, I'm lonely. Something is missing." Doctor shrugs behind the wheel, smiles very simply and openly at me.

"That's how it was with the children too. It was an awareness of their presence all the time. I stepped in when I could, when it was necessary. But it's believing God all the way and walking on that Word.

"And they are all with us now. We must have done something right. Donnie is married, has two kids, is a public school principal in Wisconsin. He's ready to come here anytime we're ready to open up a Christian Day School. He and his wife, Wanda, stand with this ministry.

"Karen and Mary too. They're both married now. Karen to Jim Martin, an academician, who has his Ph.D. from the University of Wisconsin and teaches history at Rutgers University. They have fellowships in their home. She does a lot of my editing, rewriting; works with me however and whenever she is able. She has a sharp mind. She knows my head. She's got a little girl, Darcy.

"Mary has three children. Her husband, John Somerville has his Ph.D. from Ohio State University and is a football coach at Princeton University. They're ready to come here to work with the ministry whenever we're ready to have them. They all get together — Karen, Mary and their families and have fellowships together. They live pretty close to each other in New Jersey now.

"But it's the same for them as for everyone else. They know the principles of the Word. I taught them what I knew. If they do them, it works. When they don't follow the principles, they blow it. Just like everyone else, just like you or me. God is no respecter of persons." Doctor breaks into a joyful laugh, his response to any phrase from the Word of God. He rejoices to say it or hear it. A few moments of silence pass between us. He has said what he has to say about his family. After a pause, I return to the growth of the ministry.

"But how did you get from there — from teaching your family and local Ohio people — to the outreach today? After all, there are people from New York and California, from Kansas and Alaska now. How did it go from that local, family operation to the limbs and branches of the tree now?" I ask, bringing us back to the sixties.

"There were a lot of people who came and went. I've mentioned some of their names to you. But the two important events that broke open the outreach throughout the country were the filming of the class in 1967 and my trip to California in 1968 where I first met the hippie believers. Those two happenings were the key.

"Back in 1961, I had a vision of doing the 'Power for Abundant Living' Class on 16mm sound-color film. So I began working my mind, everytime I taught that class, on producing the film.

"In about 1963, I tried once to raise the money, but it blew. People just didn't share my vision. So I took another route. Around that time we had a TV program in Lima called 'The Teacher.' We did black and white video tape. I loved working on camera. It's hard work, but I loved it. However, the films were of very poor quality. We couldn't really use them again.

"A couple of years later Dave Anderson came on the scene and asked to see those films. I was embarrassed, but I let him use them. He found them fantastic attention-getters. They could really communicate. Film is a great media, involving two of your senses, and Dave saw that potential. He and Bob Wierwille saw the vision. They raised part of the money and really spread the vision of the film.

"That was only the beginning though. The making of that film took the greatest amount of discipline and renewed mind for two months before we went into the studio and for the time we were shooting.

"The actual filming took twelve days. But there are no words in my vocabulary to describe it. We filmed in 28-minute segments, and everytime before I walked out on camera, I had almost completely memorized what I would do in that time — the charts, the scriptures, everything.

"We did as much as three and a half to four hours of filming in one day. The first day, the lights burned both my eyes. They were too bright. I looked right into 8000 watts all the time. By 2 a.m. after the first day's shooting, I couldn't get them open. They were swollen shut.

"We talked to Dr. Collier Powell and he told Dotsie that we'd better stop or I'd be blind for the rest of my life.

"The second day, I went back, and we put in a whole day. But the third day, I couldn't go, couldn't open my eyes. The next day the camera man changed the lighting so it wasn't so bright, and I went back on. We still did those 28-minute segments, but between sessions Dotsie would put ice cubes on my eyes, and Donna would read the next session to me. Then in ten to thirty minutes I'd be ready and I'd go on again.

"Every half hour I was totally soaked from the heat which went as high as 95 degrees. The air conditioning system couldn't run during filming. It's like every other thing I do — Satan fights like crazy. But you make up your mind: God's the majority and that's it.

"When we finished for the day, I'd walk off that set, put on an old shirt, go in the camper and lie down with more ice cubes on my eyes. Then all night I'd have ice cubes too. At 8 a.m. I'd get up. At 8:30 Emma Schroer, the make-up lady, came in and by 10:30 we'd leave for Dayton. We took our own camper and cars and our own food. We had to have everything absolutely ready for those twelve days. The charts alone took over 200 man-hours. The last few days of filming some people stayed up all night, night after night, getting those charts ready to go for the next day.

"I was on camera for 36 hours, edited to 33 hours, but it was a fantastic team effort. We all had the vision. Everyone just threw himself into it. Like Emogene Allen, Howard's wife, she ran the dolly with the camera on it. Howard did all the sound. Emma Schroer did my make-up every morning. Dotsie was in charge of the wardrobe and the set, got that all dusted every morning before we went on. Thelma Polei planned the charts. Helene Richey was in charge of the lettering done on the charts at Headquarters. Donna Randall was on the clapboard and kept and checked all the records. Velma Stork from the office saw to all our physical needs — running errands, taking care of the meals. And Peter Wade, the man who came here from Australia that summer of 1967, was the director of the film."

Doctor laughs suddenly, his entire face lighting up. Leaning forward over the steering wheel, he says: "He's the one who on one of the days we were filming went to pick up the letters for our charts. The guy in the shop asked him what he needed all those letters for. So Peter told him we were making a 36-hour film. The guy wanted to know who would want to see such a long film. Peter said to him, 'You don't know our ticket agent.'" Doctor chuckles again, his eyes sparkling.

"That film plus research in the holy spirit field are the greatest blessing to anybody who wants to know the Word of God and the power in His Word. They just lay it out to you. The work's been done — the research and putting it into a shape that communicates it — we've just got to reach the people with it now.

"That film really made possible the tremendous growth of the ministry. With it we could start many classes separately. I could go out, and the film could go out. I didn't have to be there, and that's when the blossoming really began.

"The film was made the fall of 1967. January, 1968, is when I went to California. Oh, it wasn't my first time in California. We had some work here and there, but nothing really significant at that time. But I would make trips like that to see our people, to see how they were getting along from time to time.

"We had a couple, Chuck and JoAnn Snider, from Ohio who had taken the 'Power for Abundant Living' Class and had moved to California. They had a small fellowship of believers near San Jose, and at that time they were the only ones standing in that area.

"The day before I left to go out there, I saw an article in *Christian Life* magazine. The truth is I never read *Christian Life*. I used to get it, look over the titles and pictures and throw it into the wastebasket. But that particular time, I was led to look through that magazine, and I saw in it an article about a group of young hippie Christians doing missionary work in Haight-Ashbury. I read it, and Father said, 'Put it into your briefcase.'

"When I got there, I told Chuck Snider I wanted to go down to Haight-Ashbury and explore, and he was ready. We went to see John MacDonald, a dyed-in-the-wool Baptist minister. And after I'd bugged him with questions for a while to get to know the facts, he suggested I go to a place called the 'Living Room,' a Christian house in Haight-Ashbury. So we all went.

"It was sort of surprising. A big table in the middle of a room. Guys sitting around, some with Bibles opened. I didn't know anything about pot, but I knew some of them were high. There was a back room with mattresses all over the floor. It was something.

"We waited there until Ted Wise came. He was the leader of that particular place. We got acquainted, and then he invited me to Novato, a place called the House of Acts, for supper and to their meeting that night.

"I did that. I went with him. We got there. The women were in the kitchen: Sandi Heefner, Judy Doop and Ted's wife. It was interesting because they were mixing up stuff — a big green salad in a bowl, bread, doing a whole trip.

"I don't know how many we had around the table — maybe 16 — and then the men came home, Steve Heefner and Jimmy Doop. They had just spent the day witnessing in Haight-Ashbury.

"We all had supper together. The women cleaned the table and the men yakked. And finally we got around to the Word. The discussion centered around the Holy Spirit. They'd been reading the book of Acts, and I asked them if they wanted me to teach them the Holy Spirit. They were hungry, but skeptical.

"It was 2 a.m. by the time I finished teaching from the book of Acts. Then they all got into a circle, and I started to lead them into speaking in tongues. None of them had spoken in tongues.

"The most interesting thing was how they all fought over the Word — Steve and Ted and Jim. They'd argue. I'd let them, then I'd give them the Word. Then they'd argue some more. I'd go on to another verse.

"Later on Chuck told me it was the most fantastic night he'd ever witnessed, seeing the Spirit of God move, leading men and women into receiving the holy spirit. It was a great night. And I saw many things there too.

"The people I'd been with before had never been really open and honest. I'm talking about the church people, the denominational types. But these young people were. If they didn't like you, they told you. And if they did like you, they told you. They didn't cover up and lie as much as the Establishment, even though they had their own prejudices.

"They could have been smoking pot, but they didn't do it in my presence. And I liked especially the tenderness among them. You see, they themselves had previously been on sex and dope, so they didn't find fault with everything all the time. They'd hug and kiss each other and that I liked. They were always affectionate. I saw a lot that I liked there.

"After I went home, I told the Board of Trustees about my experience. I knew the hippies were hungry and I knew that my teaching the Word to them would feed them. So we invited the whole House of Acts here for Summer School. We said we'd pay, and they'd be on a work scholarship. They all copped out except Steve and Sandi and their son, Stevie.

"I liked them all. I thought they were wonderful — free and honest. But I saw their congestion, their lack of knowledge, lack of grounding in the Word; and I knew that their communal living could not survive. They had kids, families. I thought every one of them was open to hearing the greatness of God's Word. But they never expressed it. I knew they'd never be satisfied, never really have the answers till they knew the accuracy of the Word of God.

"Steve was here for Summer School. It was quite a time for us, a change in the atmosphere — long hair, a full beard, different clothes. He was like lots of the young people today. He didn't know how to work. But I knew you had to have discipline, self-discipline, to really work that Word and learn. If you can't work in a field or dig a ditch for a day, what kind of discipline would you have working the Word of God?

"We kept encouraging them. They were only planning to stay two weeks, but they ended up staying the summer. Then they went back and started talking. They must have talked a lot because the following January a bunch of them came in from California to take the class — Howie Yeremian, Jim Doop, Kurt Cushing. There were others too, and they really got turned on.

"That's when the momentum of the ministry really picked up among a new group of people, young people, unaffiliated, street people, many of whom had not been raised in a particular denomination or church. We had hit a whole new audience. They had much less difficulty believing because they didn't have all those years of wrong teaching to get rid of first.

"That next summer, 1969, we had 25 people from California. One of them was Donnie Fugit who after Summer School went down to Kansas and opened up a tremendous work in Wichita. One of the students he spoke to was Tina Ranyak from Rye, New York. She went home to Rye and opened up the work on the East Coast. Now there's a limb, The Way East, in Rye.

"And it was the summer before, in 1968, that the work opened up at East Carolina University in North Carolina. Late that same summer we had the film all ready to go. We could never have kept up with the pace of growth without the film.

"Then Johnny Townsend, another young man who had the class in the army, came here that summer in 1969. He stayed here two years. Like so many of these young people, he'd rather read than work. He learned the Word, and he learned to work and study here. He'd spoil this, spoil that, and then he'd learn. Now he heads the state of Kansas, and he is the spiritual coordinator of the Western Region.

"It's like stepping stones — one person to another. There are lots of Christians around, but they don't know what they have in Christ. If someone comes into the ministry, we don't drop them, we stick with them. We never kick anyone out. They kick themselves out, if they want to go. But they're always welcome back.

"Sometimes people leave. And you wonder why you ever teach anybody — people you've poured your whole soul into. They hear something, then they want to go it alone. It's still just mainly an ego trip for them because it's how they look to other men that counts to them. They are not standing back in utter amazement of God's Word come hell or high water.

"When that happens it just tears my heart out. But I have that Word so deep in my soul that if nobody else believes it, I would still stand.

"I could be right on 98 things out of a hundred and people would be against me because I'm wrong in two. And so they go. It's always a spiritual fight to stay on top of it.

"It was in that great growth after 1968, among the young people, where I saw the need for leaders — people strong in knowledge and zeal, people with commitment prepared to handle ministries and responsibilities.

"We started the first Way Corps then, the fall of 1969, especially for that purpose, to prepare leaders. There were nine of them — some married, some single, younger and older. They stayed till the spring, and then I gave them the privilege of leaving. You see, they never got it together among themselves. They didn't have that commitment, that discipline. They just kept fighting among themselves. But you know what? They're all standing today, all but one, and she'll be back. She'll get tired of messing around after a while. And she'll be back because there's nowhere else to go after you have seen the greatness of the Word.

"I guess the time wasn't ripe. But we all learned some things in the process. When the first Corps left, I'd really had enough; but we still had a need for leaders — faithful men. You don't turn into a faithful man who is able also to teach others overnight. It takes time.

"That's why we have the two-year training here for the Corps. They get right to the heartbeat of the ministry, to see it from the inside-out. They have two years to study, work, teach, witness and just plain live together.

"If you can't get a bunch of Christians to live together right here — where all their needs are met, where all the people around them love them — how are they going to make it out in the field, out in the world, in the outreach where they are bombarded by negatives and doubts by the people around them? If they can't live in love and peace here, where are they going to live in love and peace? That's what the Corps prepares them for. They build up that love of God in them and then take it with them everywhere they go.

"This second year Corps — they're terrific. There are nine of them who came in the fall of 1970 and will graduate this year in August after the Rock of Ages. Then they're ready to lead in the field. That'll be a great day. They've stood through thick and thin. They've grown, and they really understand this ministry." Doctor shakes his head, and I see from his profile his eyes glistening. He clears his throat and goes on.

"The Ambassadors is a similar program to develop leaders, faithful men, people with commitment right out on the field. It's like Jesus said, 'The harvest truly *is* plenteous, but the labourers *are* few.' Well, we're allowing real laborers to develop. It's just beautiful.

"The first wave of ambassadors went out after the Rock of Ages last summer. Then we had two more waves. The next wave will go out after the Rock of Ages, August, 1972. There they are, young people with commitment out on the field. They'll either stand and get stronger, or they'll fall. If they stand, they are stedfast." Doctor talks faster picking up enthusiasm and excitement.

"And this new campaign we're talking about now, it's a way to open up new areas. We're just holding forth that Word of God. Holding it forth, rightly divided. Then the people who hear can choose — either they say it's a bunch of baloney or they believe.

"God said He'd teach me His Word like it hadn't been known since the first century if I would teach it to others. And that's how I think: How can we teach it to others, make it live?" Doctor shakes his head, his face cast in seriousness.

"Yes, the day God made me this promise was the greatest day of my life, that and the day I received the holy spirit because they were both centers of reference for my learning truth and error. You have to have a center of reference out-side of yourself to learn. And no matter who you talk to, you always learn. Those two encounters with Him are as real to me today as my talking with you right now.

"I'm doing my best day by day to put it together, to know the work and to carry it out. I'm going over all my men in the ministry to see. We're right on the threshold of this thing. It's going to skyrocket nationally. We have to move people up, give them responsibilities, let them prove themselves, pre-pare the way for the growth. We have to reorganize our work to be even more efficient to be on top of it all structurally when it happens. But God will supply all our needs.

"This whole thing will change. I see the handwriting on the wall. I see how that Word has transformed the lives of people, has taken them from death into life. It's just so big. It's like that first warm day in spring when everything is about to burst open and bloom.

"Things are so great now — like last Sunday night at the meeting with people open to the Word of God like flowers to the sun. They'd have stayed all night if I had taught them. They know the greatness of the Word. You see, the Bible explains everything — ESP, spiritualism, phenomena, sick-ness, death, everything. The Bible explains all those, but ESP or spiritualism can't explain the Word or the power of God available to us.

"Once you've seen the greatness of that Word live and people live for each other, it's just the sweetest fellowship this side of heaven. You're never the same after that class.

And when you're the teacher, why, everytime you teach you see it bigger, and you deepen in your understanding of the love of God.

"But you get tired. The other night I was so tired I couldn't even find the books of the Bible. When you work so hard, everyone loves you; but when you get right down to it, it's you and God to handle that Word, and you have to make it live with the renewed mind. That's what's really important. And other of life's tinsel just doesn't count against the greatness of the Word of God.

"This is the greatest loving ministry in the world — and the most lonesome walk. I suppose it's like being an athlete. In football, there are eleven; in basketball, five; but when you teach, it's just you and Daddy.

"Lots of people love you for the Word you teach, but when it comes right down to it, it's just you. You stand and you walk. You teach what they can take. And sometimes you know a whole lot more. Things you could open your heart on, you never do, to those depths of perception. You go so far. You know the abundance available and the Father says, 'That's all folks, end of show.' And it's something you cannot describe to people. Just you and Father know."

Doctor slows the car down through New Knoxville. His face is serious, tender. His eyebrows drawn together. We cruise by Adolph's Restaurant and other quaint, familiar places. It seems we've gone around the world, been away for years or even decades. Shafts of golden sunlight burn through the billows of honey-edged clouds. The sky has gained in height, the low clouds have dispersed. The wind has fallen to a whisper in the heavens, a vast blanket of peace covers the earth.

"Well, honey, we're almost home," Dr. Wierwille remarks with a heavy sigh that sounds like relief. "We've traveled a long way today." We turn off Route 29 past The Way sign and up the road to The Way farm. We have come home. "The longest road is the return home, but it's the best when you get there."

Along the slender black-top road and across the bridge in the distance, a dozen figures clothed in navy sweatsuits are running toward us. Doctor slows the car down, laughing and smiling.

"That's my Corps," he says affectionately. "They're my kids." We drive slowly toward them and through them. Their flushed faces streaked with red patches break into sudden smiles. Panting, they put in that extra push, run by us, waving at Doctor's window. It must be just after 4:30, I calculate. That's when the Corps members run in the afternoons. They'll go to the end of the road and back, a good mile or maybe more.

Over the bridge, we turn into the driveway marked "Entrance," and Doctor pulls up slowly in front of his house. He straightens his shoulders as though casting the whole past of the afternoon off his back, and turns towards me. "Come on into my office. It's not suppertime yet, and I have a few phone calls to make. You can sit in and see what's happening," he invites me and then steps out of the car. A chorus of barking sounds out from the dog kennels. Doctor strides up the cement path, and we walk across the veranda to his office. Everything is as we left it — people working, needs being met, things being done. Everything went on without us.

Doctor holds open the door to his office. "It's time to shift gears again," he says, breaking into a burst of merry laughter. Even before we step across the threshold, the phone rings. Two telephones stand on the broad windowsill.

"Which phone was it?" Doctor asks, shrugs and laughs. A ring again. He grabs one receiver, but the phone continues to ring. "Well, you can't be right all the time," he shrugs, picking up the other receiver. "I sure couldn't tell. Hello," and he has launched into a conversation, waving me into a chair, talking, exhorting and comforting the person who is on the other end.

On the phone Doctor discusses buying a house in Wichita. I pick up the conversation. It must be John Townsend if it's from Wichita.

"It sounds good. What are the mortgage arrangements? (Pause) The money down is good, but work it out so you can pay the whole thing off in a couple of months. (Pause) Okay. (More discussion on financial arrangements, thorough approach to details, Doctor brings up every possible question in the matter.) Then enthusiastically, "You're just beautiful. Bless your heart." Doctor drops the receiver back into the cradle, slaps his knee with a laugh.

"That was Johnny Townsend in Wichita. He wants to buy a house. They need one and they have found a good one. Do you know what he was concerned about?" Doctor asks, looking at me inquisitively. "He's concerned that if they buy that house, they won't be sending as much money as usual back to Headquarters. Bless his heart. Everyone in his area is tithing. He sends back more money than anyone, and he's concerned about us. Well, bless God. I sure get a kick out of my Johnny."

Dr. Wierwille is back in the swing of his office. His raincoat is draped over the bronze statue of Lincoln thoughtfully holding a scroll. The office is good-sized with picture windows on two walls overlooking the rolling lawns. Outside one window a huge male mulberry tree stands, a complex of limbs, branches and twigs growing off a straight black trunk. It looks like The Way Tree to me. Such a multitude of little twigs, bare today, but blooming with leaves tomorrow.

Doctor is flipping through his telephone file. He finds a number. Adjusting his dark-rimmed glasses, he dials. (Pause) His face brightens. "Hi, Steve, how are you? Aren't you wonderful!" Doctor is enjoying himself, as he always does when he deals directly with people, or whatever he is doing for that matter. You have to shift gears. That's the renewed mind.

"What about the room for the Advanced Class coming up?" he queries. "You're beautiful. And how's my Sandi?" He talks laughing and smiling, transmitting his exuberance over the telephone wires. He runs through arrangements for the Advanced Class in Rye, finishes, signs off and goes on to the next call.

Then it's San Francisco, Denver, Las Vegas. Every call is short — business and blessing. No time is wasted on nonsense. He works out some arrangements for "The Way Presents" opening up in California on April 2, two weeks from now. Very quickly details are worked out, verified. He'll stop in Denver and Las Vegas on his way to Oakland. In each place he'll teach one evening, bless the saints, build up the Body.

It's California for a week, then Rye for three weeks, then home, then somewhere else. That is how it looks now, but you never know what else is coming up. My head is swimming with the pace. I can hardly fit all the details into my head. But Doctor is right on top of it, molding the schedule into shape with his booming, enthusiastic voice.

After talking to Las Vegas, he laughs jubilantly again, "I just called to tell the guy when I was coming, and he just about hit the ceiling. They get so turned on. It's wonderful." He pauses to look up the next number. But before he can dial, the buzzer on the intercom breaks the momentary stillness. It's Rhoda, his secretary. I gather she wants to bring in correspondence for him to sign before supper. "Bring it over. You're just beautiful." He hangs up, swings his black leather desk chair back next to the telephones.

Our afternoon together slides through my mind. The Doctor could never have had time to talk without interruption in the office the way he did this afternoon while we were gone. Good thing he took me for a ride. That's how it is in the office — people, decisions, a continual stream of interruptions, the constant work of the ministry. That is his life.

He is looking for another number. Muffled from somewhere outside, I hear the voice over the PA system make the familiar announcement: "Ten minutes till supper, ten minutes till supper. Will somebody please ring the bell." And then the bell clangs, two times, three, four.

It's been a long day. I'm ready for supper. No, I'm ready for bed. My head is swimming with facts, figures, memories, pictures, impressions, conclusions, observations, emotions, excitement and fatigue. I stand up.

"You go ahead to supper, honey. Tell them to start without me. I have some more calls to make right now." Doctor addresses me with a paternal concern. The phone rings again.

"Dr. Wierwille," he speaks into the receiver. "Well, hi, honey, God bless." And he's talking, listening, nodding his head. His words fade abruptly in my ears, as I close the door behind me, walking to the Biblical Research Center for supper.

*Evening* _____

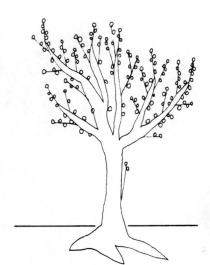

*Evening*

*T*he wind has ceased, and a quiet warmth is rising from the earth overcoming the chill of the air. High in the sky, a few clouds move monumentally calm, unperturbed, bathed by the golden rays of the late afternoon sun. Looks like it will clear up before tomorrow. Looks like it's getting warmer — spring is on its way.

Two or three figures move slowly in the direction of the Biblical Research Center. The short walk soothes my mind. I make my way through the basement, in among the tables and flop down on the couch, my eyelids heavy.

The dining room is quiet. People come in, a murmuring of voices, a calm in the atmosphere. Everyone has put in a whole day. It's great to stop, to get together like this at five o'clock, to fellowship and eat, to see those smiling faces.

Opening my eyes, I find myself looking right into the brown and lively eyes of Paul Vergilio, the leader of the music group "Selah." Beside me on the other side is Dave Buschman, tall, blonde, his hands still blackened with freshly washed off grease. He must have been heavy into some machine repairs today.

Each of them smiles back at me in turn. And the unheard voice behind the smile is clear and warm, saying: 'I love you. You're just the greatest.' It's the love of God. Does it every time. My heart melts and weariness slips off my shoulders like an old coat. I cast it away, and turn back to Paul.

"Say, Paul, how did you ever get into music?" I ask, suddenly interested.

"The way I got into everything. I just taught myself. I was an orphan from Italy after the war. I was one of the lucky ones. I was adopted into an Italian-American family, and I spent a lot of time in Philadelphia. I just taught myself music. I liked it so I did it. I guess that's how you learned writing," he finishes.

"Yes," I reflect. "I just did it because I love doing it.

"That's it," Paul picks up. "I just dig doing it. I guess you have to love what you're doing. Then you've got the patience to learn to do it well. Patience — that's a key. If you love what you do, it gives you patience. Now I could never sit down and write a book. I'd freak out." Paul laughs.

"I tried to teach myself to play the guitar once," I recount. "I even seriously considered taking lessons. I'd have loved to learn because I love to sing. I tried, but my fingers got sore, and I just couldn't make it sound like anything. I gave it up; but writing, now that's different. That's great. I can really get into it."

And then Dave joins in the conversation, "Yeh, that's how I got to be a mechanic. I really wanted to do something with my hands, work with my hands. Motors and machines always turned me on, so I studied it in school and then in college. Now I work on the cars here. I can repair anything.

"You know, I can listen to tape teachings when I do some things. But when I start working on an engine, I can't listen to a tape because I get so deep into my work. I just can't hear anything else. I really concentrate," Dave laughs, holding up his washed hands still darkened by hard-to-remove grease.

I laugh and add, "And if my car breaks down, I'm lost. I can hardly tell the window from the bumper. I don't know a thing. I have to call somebody. I'm sure glad someone has that kind of knowhow."

The room has filled imperceptably, and Nancy, the hostess, is calling us to take our seats. "Praise the Lord," goes through my head. Here we are on the couch, the three of us — a musician, a writer and a mechanic. We all work with our hands and with our minds. We produce entirely different products. We each work with our hands a thing that is good, the thing we love to do. And we are all members of the same Body, all in Christ. God opens doors for us so that we can meet each others' needs and bless the Body by doing the thing we love to do best. Where else can there be such an opportunity to grow in love and skill?

Everyone selects a chair at a table. It doesn't matter where I sit. I slip over to the nearest chair, hear the blessing and sit down. And then I look at the supper — my favorite. I had been so involved I didn't even notice it till now. How good can God be? — bowls of steaming apple and cherry crisp, thick slabs of crust peeking out from amid the juicy cooked fruit, two bowls of vanilla ice cream in rich creamy mounds, and a bowl of raw cashews. Pure dessert for supper — that's abundance.

It's a quiet supper today or I'm not registering much. Everyone must be hungry, eating, enjoying it. I don't say much, but listen. Dr. Spencer is here from West Virginia, visiting for a day or two. I've met him before, didn't know he was here today. A physician in his fifties, he took the class a year ago. Dr. Spencer is talking.

"I just knew there must be something," he is saying. "I just didn't know *how* with a capital *H*. I had this strong Presbyterian background that said don't pray for the sick because it might be God's will they don't get well. So I thought, 'Heck, why pray.' But when I really knew God's Word, I knew His will was health for everyone. I just knew I could pray for the sick and God would make things come to pass. And what changes I've seen since then!

"I had a cardiac myself not long ago. I had it and now I'm completely healed. We learned in medical school that a fear of death is a symptom of cardiac condition. Well, of course, fear of death. People get what they believe. Fear is negative believing. Next thing, they're dead. But when mine happened, I was assured I wouldn't die. I believed positively and was completely healed." Dr. Spencer shakes his head in relief, as though he had just had a narrow escape.

"That Word of God is so fantastic that once you get it and believe, you just want to share it with everybody to tell them all it's done for you in your life.

"I've been in the ministry a year now. I started out by being a hunter of men. You know, you watch them, stalk them, then you get them in your sights and let them have it with both barrels.

"But I've been seeing more and more what the Word says: You've got to be a fisher of men, like Peter. Every fish is different. You put out the bait, and it's different for different fish. You put it out, and our bait is the best. You dangle it here, tease a little, get the hunger up. Then when you get a fish on the line, you pull it in. Some you play with. Some get away from you, but they keep coming back, and you just gotta keep the bait there all the time.

"So that's what I've been working on lately — being an expert fisherman, not a hunter — and it's great." Dr. Spencer breaks off. Someone else picks it up. Conversation meanders around our table. Supper is delicious. The apple crisp hot, cooled by cold ice cream melts in my mouth.

And then with quiet force, Doctor comes down the stairs. A wave of responses fills the air, a kind of running excitement electrifies the dining room. We all know that when Doctor is around, we're going to learn something. We all sit up with expectation.

He walks over to his place beside Mrs. Wierwille, shaking his head at all offers of food, but accepting a cup of coffee. He seats himself up on the back of his chair. A hush sweeps over the louder sounds in the room.

"Okay. Are there any announcements tonight?" Doctor looks over the group. Pat, the bearded carpenter, raises his hand.

"Don't forget the staff twig fellowship tonight. It's a sharing type of trip. So bring your hearts and your Bibles if you want to. Right after supper in Trailer 8. Oh, yes, and all guests are invited to this fellowship, that includes the visiting ambassadors, and you too, Dr. Spencer." Pat finishes and sits down.

"Thanks, Pat. Who else? Nobody? Nothing to share? You mean to tell me, I go away for an afternoon and nothing happens here?" Doctor pushes.

"Well then, I'll tell you something. I just got off the phone with a lady from Columbus, Ohio. This lady wants to give us a house in Columbus. She inherited money, but she doesn't get it in her hands till two years from now. Some kind of provision in the will. But she called me today to say they are giving her $600 per month for rent and $10,000 to furnish a house in Columbus. That's not bad. We can get a pretty good house for that.

"She told her lawyers and executors: 'What's the difference? In two years I'll do what I dang well please with that money, and tomorrow I'll do what I dang well please with that money. So what? The real difference is that right now that money's helping nobody. It's just sitting in the bank. And if it weren't for The Way, my daughter would be dead today. So I want The Way to have the use of some of that money now.'

"That's how she laid it out to them. So they went through a lot of red tape, and finally they're letting her have money for monthly rent and money to furnish a house for The Way in Columbus. That's pretty good. Praise the Lord. So now we're looking for a house down in Columbus." Doctor raises his eyebrows enthusiastically, smiling from one to another person around the room. There's a wave of happy reactions, and then Meg's voice says simply, "You see, Dr. Wierwille, you came into some money today. Remember how your mustache itched at lunch?"

"Why I never thought of that, Meg. Must have been a revelation," he concludes slapping his knee and laughing along with everyone else. "Whatever comes to me, I give it to

The Way. I don't need any money. My needs are met. That's wonderful. Is there anything else?" No one answers.

"I got another one for you then, since you're all so quiet — especially for my Corps. You're all going witnessing tonight in Sidney. You leave here at 7:30. It's time you got out into the world, look around and see what's happening out there. Oh, we know the world. We know it from the Word. But I want you to go out and have a look. You might be getting rusty or something. So you can get moving tonight. Sidney, 7:30. Got it? Craig, you take care of the cars — I guess we'll need three or four.

"Anything else that has to be said before this illustrious group leaves? Then you may roll it away. God bless and have a beautiful evening." Doctor finishes on the upbeat, gives us a wave of his hand and walks out of the dining hall.

Conversation picks up, laughter, the clamor of roll away — silver into old coffee cans, dishes being passed. Even though it's before six o'clock, the evening stretches before me as though we were beginning the day again, as though it were the womb of the morning.

Pulling myself out of my seat, I pick up my notebook and start back to Trailer 5. I could fall over and sleep now or just be alone and read my Bible. I really would like to go witnessing with the Corps. And there's the twig fellowship in Trailer 8. Take it one at a time.

My mind is full of all that happens in a day in the Body of Christ. All that happens. But it's just another day. Another day the Lord has made. Let us rejoice and be glad in it. But a myriad of thoughts crowd into my brain, shouldering each other, pushing each other around — bossy thoughts.

How do you write a book about this? How do you put it on paper? There's just so much to see, so much to say. There's so much happening. How do you capture joy or love in words? How do you make the high of the Sunday night meeting live on a printed page? Or how do you describe that serious commitment, that inaudible sound of listening at the Tuesday night Corps meeting? And how can you put forty or fifty people in one book, how do you tell the stories of each life, how do you recount the miracle that brought each one from death into life? And how do you enumerate the numerous little miracles that follow different members of the Body through one day, or a week? And how do you show a blessing? After all, you can't see it, only the effects. Where am I going to put it all?

The thoughts hammer through my head. Well, that's the human mind for you — your greatest enemy if you don't get it under control, or your most fabulous and versatile multi-purpose tool. I'll go to the fellowship. Can't sleep now anyway with all these thoughts bugging me. But I won't say anything.

I leave my notebook in Trailer 5, pick up my large black, wide-margin Bible, each page covered with minute notes, and start up the path to Trailer 8. Wish I could leave my quandary behind, I'm thinking. And how do you tell it like it is about Dr. Wierwille, his wife, his family, the greater family here on the farm? How can you say it all? My thoughts pile up into a massive mountain right in the middle of my path. I can't climb over it, and I surely can't see my way around.

I know, I know. I'm more than a conqueror in every situation. That's what the Word says. God always causes us to triumph in Christ. Always. Look at it. Either it's the truth or it's a lie. If it's the truth, just believe. It's the truth, and I believe it. But my mind shouts back across the din of competing thoughts: "How? How are you going to do it?"

I can't answer that question now. My mind is a blank, but I'm glad I decided to go to the twig meeting. I sure need to hear something, be reminded of something. I really have a need. See what happens. God says He will supply all our needs according to His riches in glory through Christ Jesus. Well, God, I sure don't see how, so you have to show me. And you have to show me simple so I'll understand.

In Trailer 8 Pat and Nancy Johnson, the young marrieds from Wichita on staff here, are already seated in the living room. Susan, the girl who sews, and Brenda, the black girl with the big smile from the Main Office Trailer, are on the couch. The atmosphere is homey, peaceful, light. They are jolly, laughing about something. I fall on the couch beside Brenda, who squeezes my hand affectionately and then returns to the conversation with Pat.

Two minutes pass. Bob Nixon and Danny Stockemer walk in. Both are W.O.W. ambassadors in here from the field to do some special work, spring planting, I believe. I suddenly remember the announcements from another day, yesterday, or the day before, but I just haven't had a chance to speak with either of them.

The room is simply furnished, neat, a cuckoo clock on the wall, an old brass bound trunk serving as a coffee table beside the couch. Another knock. Angie and Paul walk in. It's only their second day here, but already I notice changes in their faces — a softness in their smiles, a certain relaxation in the facial muscles, something peaceful and tender creeping in behind the eyes.

The cuckoo clock announces six o'clock. Pat clears his throat, opens the meeting with a short prayer and then starts rapping.

"Well, folks, we have another special meeting tonight, Bob and Danny and I, so we'll only be here an hour, till seven. Does anyone know where Claudettee is? Or Tricia?"

"They went to a fellowship in Lima. I think Claudettee is teaching there tonight." Brenda informs us.

"Okay, that's great. And I want to introduce the new people, maybe some of you didn't get a chance to meet them yet." Pat introduces everyone and then continues.

"This is a sharing time. What's on your hearts, folks? Did you learn anything today or this week?" Pat looks around at us, his face lighted with a smile both shy and bold. He's only nineteen, but it's been a long road home. I flash on the fact that he was heavy into drugs — heroin for over a year. He would have had it if he hadn't found The Way. And look at him now, leading the meeting, loving us all, ready to talk, ready to listen, cracking his Kansas jokes. It just makes me smile on the inside — what that Word of God can do. It's beyond me. Just don't see how, but I know it does.

Bob Nixon, thinning blonde hair and wire-rimmed glasses, launches in, and we all listen.

"Well, I learned something today, while I was digging the ditch out by the Wierwille house. It really blessed me, and I'd like to share it with you." Bob clears his throat.

"Well, Danny and I had a long ditch to dig and it was hard work. And what I learned again was that you have to keep the goal foremost in your mind. It's heavy. You can't look at each shovelful of dirt. There were so many, one after another. The ditch was three feet deep and I don't know how long.

"But you have to keep that goal in mind all the time. The goal was to get it dug, to lay the pipe in, to fill it up and to have that water flowing through it. That was getting it done. You see, when I looked at each shovelful, each one became so weighty, so heavy, I just slowed down, got tired. But when I kept my eyes on the goal, on getting the job done, then each shovelful became so light, so easy, just the means to the end. The goal is the end and it's to the glory of God." Bob stops talking and regards all of us with a smile.

I listen completely absorbed, and then suddenly, it's like a burglar alarm system being tripped off in my mind. I wake up. I know that he is talking to me, even though he doesn't know it. I know that this is what I needed to hear right now.

I came here with a need tonight — plagued by annoyances and doubts about how I'm going to put this place into words, about the immensity of the task, the profusion of material. Well, you heard him — keep your eyes on the goal. Don't look at each shovelful, just get it done. Even though I was not going to say anything, I know now I have to speak up.

"Listen," I blurt out, louder than I had expected. "I've been really bugged today. About this book — I don't know how to write it — there's so much material, so much to say. I'm just overwhelmed," I finish. There, it's out. Get honest. "I just can't get started with it, it seems so immense. I don't even know why I'm bothering you with this stuff. It's so silly. I should be able to handle it myself. I'm just annoyed with myself. What do I do?" I finish plaintively, looking around the room a little sheepishly.

Everyone listens till I am through. Pat and Danny regard me with understanding. Love without boldness is smother love. There is no pity or sympathy in their facial expressions.

"Stand," Pat says. "Just stand on what the Word says. You know where the hassles are coming from. Kick them out."

"Walk," Danny says, his brown eyes intense. He shrugs his shoulders a little and smiles warmly. His head is covered with tight brown curls, like a nobleman in a Renaissance painting I once saw.

"I wasn't even going to say anything tonight," I continue. "It's such a drag. But when Bob told us what he learned today, about keeping that goal in mind, I just knew he was saying it to me. It's what I needed to hear. I just forgot about the goal and got carried away by the task. I knew it was a trick. I just couldn't throw it off."

There is a silence, then Danny leans forward in his chair and addresses me.

"Let me tell you something else about that ditch. I was out there working with Bob today too, and I learned something, or relearned something, really neat." He nods his head, his curls moving about his face in time to his enthusiasm.

"We worked all day. We dug the main part of the ditch, and then we had to dig a hole to make a connection with another pipe below it. We weren't sure where that connection was, so we thrust a stick into the ground, till it hit something. We figured that it must be the other pipe. So we dug there, three feet down, and then we found it wasn't the pipe we needed. It was a large stone.

"Well, this was after lunch, and the guy that knew the layout of the pipes had gone off somewhere — we didn't know where. We could have just stopped and waited around till he got back to tell us exactly where we should dig. But we decided that would be a waste of time; we'd just go on.

"You see, we had one other section of pipe to lay in conjunction with the ditch we had dug already. So we took a string, measured the best we knew how and just started digging that section out.

"Just when we got through, late in the afternoon, the guy came back. Do you know that the ditch was in exactly the right place? It was perfect. And the hole we had dug down looking for the other pipe connection — that was in the perfect position for another section of pipe that has to go in, that we didn't even know about." Danny's eyes sparkle with excitement, and he laughs, leaning back again in his chair.

"That's what I learned today. You just have to do it — whatever it is that you have to do — and believe God. If you're doing God's work, He'll just have to help you. You don't need to know how He's going to help you or why or how come. That's all His problem. You just walk out. You do it and believe God for the results." Danny's face is taut with the intensity of his communication.

"I see, I see, Danny. I knew it, but I forgot. Thank you for reminding me. It doesn't matter how I feel or what my mind tells me. I just do it, keep doing it and believe God!" I can hardly believe how simple it is. I am liberated, sprung from a subtle bondage. I'm suddenly light and free, released. I have something my mind can grasp — a rock, a foundation. It's really so easy. Put it in your mind. You do your best and God does the rest. Just do it and believe God.

A blessing washes over us as the waves of the sea wash over bathers at the beach. I am blessed. We are all blessed —

to be loved, exhorted, comforted, reminded. Praise God, the blessing washes over us, refreshes us, lightens us. We rejoice. We love each other. Praise God I came here tonight. I stated my need, and God met it through a brother.

We suddenly all smile at one another, giggle a little, laugh together. There is a lightness in the air, a lightness in our heads. Everyone has been blessed. Like children playing on the beach, the sun glistening diamonds among the grains of sand, building castles, running, jumping, falling down and getting up again, laughing and sparkling. God's love surrounds us. The waves of God's love lapping around our feet, blessing us. The waves wash over us — together, cool, peaceful. We rejoice, silly and free as children playing on the beach by the sea.

We all know here, now, in this very room that we've been blessed to the cores of our beings. Yet, there is nothing to point to, nothing to put a finger on, nothing really to see, hear, touch, smell or taste. Nothing. But we all know God's presence with us, in us and around us. God's blessing on us is more living and real than anything our senses reveal. God is spirit. God is here and now.

The meeting is in high gear. Funny, it always happens at a twig. Susan shares something. We talk. We listen. And then the cuckoo bird springs out of his door again. Pat glances up at the clock.

"Hey, we have to get to that other meeting." Pat picks up his notebook and Bible. "Listen, everyone. I'm here to serve you. If you ever need to see me or talk to me, tell me. I'm here for you. It blesses me to help you in any way I can.

"Let's have a closing prayer. Father, I thank you for your wonderful love for us, that you shed on us every minute. I just thank you for how you're always on time, for how you always meet needs when they come up, that you never let us hang around uncertain. But you let us know how much you love us — all the time, no matter how we blow it. Thank you, Father, God, for a great evening of learning, for alertness of mind and the great growth we can have through your Son Jesus Christ. Amen."

Danny, Bob and Pat get up to leave amid warm blessings and good-byes.

"What are you doing tonight, Elena?" Susan asks me. It's seven o'clock.

"I wanted to go witnessing tonight with the Corps. They're going to Sidney. But it's been a long day. I don't know if I'm up to it." I pause. "What are you doing tonight?"

"I have a lot of sewing yet to do. Lots of stuff to finish. And later tonight, I'll run, before I go to bed. It's real neat. I just love it. I just started," she finishes off in her sweet deep-

South enunciation. "But you know you can do all things. You can rest a half hour and go with the Corps at 7:30. You'll have a good time," she ends in a positive tone as we walk out the door together.

"That was a great meeting."

"Yeh, it sure met my needs. Wow, that was something. I sure needed to hear that."

I am thinking — the life of the tree is in the twigs. It's the tenderness in the twig that makes for growth. The tenderness in the twig, the love in manifestation, meeting each other's needs in the Body. Love is to meet needs. That twig meeting was living and real. We all grew individually and grew in love toward one another.

"Well, have a beautiful evening, whatever you decide to do," Susan tosses out after walking a little way with me. "Have a great evening. God bless you," she calls as she runs towards the Biblical Research Center.

"You too, Susan. God bless you," I echo as the sound of her footsteps fades in the distance.

The last red rays of the sunset glow in the western sky coloring a few lingering clouds. The sky is blue, undaunted now, covering the flat lands with gentle hues. It's going to be a clear day tomorrow. The muddy spots on the ground are glistening again. The earth is softening, the dark brown soil relaxes from freezing, turns into fertile earth. Sparrows twitter fluttering from branch to branch among the apple trees.

"Well," I am thinking, "I've got a half hour. What now, Lord?" I could sack out or go talk to someone. No, I've talked to enough people today. Sack out, there won't be time anyway. I could organize today's notes — but my head just isn't there. Or run.

Or run. Yes, I could run up the road and back, take a shower and be ready by 7:30. Only takes a few moments. If your body gets bored on you, give it something to do. I've been sitting around all day, sitting, talking and listening.

I could run. Redeem the time. Why not? Get some air in your lungs. That Susan had a good idea. It will set me in motion for the evening.

I drop off my Bible, put on my sneakers, walk out to the road. No one is to be seen. I am alone in the twilight, very small against the expanse of fields, very small against the overreaching sky.

Breaking into a slow jog, I feel that gentle air on my face, the softness of twilight in early spring, the whispering of night falling. My body follows my mind. Just do it and believe God. Keep the goal always before your eyes.

I'm breathing heavier, the air catching in my lungs, burning on the way out, my steps pounding down the empty, black-top road. No sound but my footfalls. I recall Doctor's words from the afternoon: "In football there are eleven of you, and in basketball there are five, but when you're walking the walk, or running the race, when you're standing, it's just you and God. You run it alone. But God is always with you, not because of what you feel, but because you know His Word."

My breath comes in shorter gasps, strands of sweaty hair flying in my eyes. I could stop. I could stop now. But you know, every time you set a goal and accomplish it, it's another victory for God. God is my strength. Do you believe God?

The muscles at the backs of my legs are aching, slowing me down, pulling me back. "That's okay. You won't die. God is your strength. If you can do this, you can do anything. If God is your strength now, He is your strength always." Footsteps thudding on the pavement. Stillness of the falling night. Calm brown-eyed cows gaze at me from the nearby field. Sharp gasps of heavy breathing. I think I'll cough up my lungs next step.

And I suddenly remember Cathi's teaching one night. Lovely brown curls, her large brown eyes, smiling from behind the pulpit, the sensuous curve of her jaw, a deep purple dress. She is looking straight at me and saying, "When I run, and I think I'm ready to die, and I think I'm not going to make it, I just set this picture in my mind. I just picture Jesus Christ has come back, and He's at the Biblical Research Center, waiting there for me. And then, I just forget everything else. I forget my whole body. And I just want to get there as fast as I can. I just don't care about anything else. I know I'm going to make it," a toss of her long brown curls.

Maybe He is there now waiting for me. Keep the goal before your eyes. Just do it and believe God. Maybe He'll leave if I don't step on it. Hurry up, legs.

I'm heaving, panting. The muscles are jabbing me between my shoulder blades. My mouth twitches. I can feel the blood pounding through my heart, pounding in my face. What if He is there? He could be. Hurry up.

I round the corner of the Biblical Research Center. No one anywhere to be seen. Praise the Lord. I made it. God is my strength. Just do it and believe. When you come right down to it, it's like you're an athlete running a race — it's just you and God.

I pant my way back to Trailer 5, my chest heaving uncontrollably. Empty. A quick encounter with the shower — kind of a human car wash. In and out. Dry off. Something fresh and neat to go witnessing in Sidney. It's nearly warm out. Wear something light. Light? You are the light. It's going to be great. I can't wait. Never know what the evening will drop in your lap, but you know it's going to be the best. The clock says 7:28. Closing the door behind me, I walk over to the Biblical Research Center to meet the Corps.

Promptly at 7:30, two cars are in front of the Biblical Research Center. Before I reach them, a third car draws up behind. Tall Craig, slip of paper in hand, is seating us. Some ambassadors are going too. People are flocking to the waiting cars, changed from the work clothes of the day, hair combed and brushed, ready to go out into the world, to walk a good witness.

"You go with Dave Buschman," Craig tells me, glancing on his list, then turns to the next person. "You too, Sky. That fills up his car. Why don't you guys go ahead and leave? Buschman knows where to go. We'll see you there. Bless you. Have a great, profitable evening," Craig calls after us.

Sky holds the car door. I slide into the front seat beside Dave, who is holding up a portable tape recorder above the steering wheel. When I am seated, he hands it over to me.

"Do you mind holding this? I want to play a tape on the way there. John Townsend is teaching on witnessing. It's a great tape. This will be the third time I've heard it." Dave's manner of speech is soft and gentle. I note that his hands have been thoroughly scrubbed since before supper. The grease is gone. He is wearing a clean flower-print shirt, no tie and a light jacket.

Sky slides in beside me. In back are Becky, Tina and Brian. (The latter two are both in the Way Corps and both are from Rye, New York.) Dave looks us all over.

"You all set?" he asks and then starts to drive. "Just flick the switch. Turn it up full volume, so the people in back can hear." I push the button, holding the tape recorder evenly on my lap, and the tape reels roll.

The voice speaks slowly and evenly. We all listen in silence. Dave drives. "When you're out witnessing," the voice is saying, "never argue." That's a good point, I am thinking. Sometimes it's hard — like Dr. Spencer was saying at supper tonight. You are so full of what the knowledge of God's Word has done for you, you just want to shout it from the housetops or talk someone's ear off whether he wants to listen or not. No good. Remember that: Never argue. The tape rolls on.

Night has fallen. The sky is clear, the moon rising just over the front windshield. Glowing stars scattered in the darkness — golden nailheads hammered in to hold the sky up. The car is quiet. Everyone listening. The voice talks on, teaches, instructs, cracks a few funny jokes, and we have arrived.

It's a teenage hangout in Sidney. White tile walls, booths and tables, a counter, large window. The place is over half full. It's still early in the evening. Young people crowd around several tables, cokes and loud laughter, a juke box wails mournfully, "Heartbreaker."

"We'll just stay an hour and then go to another place," Dave informs the five of us, and we split up. Sky takes a seat at the counter. Dave has already fallen into conversation with a bearded young man. Becky stands with them, lifting and listening. The others in our group, I can't even see now. They have melted into their surroundings. You can hardly tell them apart, like guerrillas in a jungle.

It's mostly a young group — early teen, thirteen, fourteen maybe, slender, growing bodies, acne. They all exhibit the same faddy styles, bluejeans, T-shirts, with clever sayings, far-out pictures. It's a young crowd — the boys stick with the boys, the girls titter with the girls. I see one or two couples, but that's all. They haven't hit the stage of pairing off yet. Their youthfulness hums with undirected energy, undefined excitement and a constant motion. The young have a beauty they don't even know.

Suddenly my eye stops on a young girl, barely passed puberty. She has a creamy face, unmolded by experience, and long straight honey-colored hair. She giggles and whispers with two or three girlfriends. She is very obviously pregnant. I *know* I have to talk with her.

She is surrounded by her little friends, giggling, cooing together, fluttering like newly-hatched birds. I know I have something to say to her, but I also see that I cannot approach her in her group. I have to get to her alone. I hover in the distance, watching the action. She rises. Three others stand up with her, and they move together, in a little flock to the counter, pick up some more sodas and return to their seats.

I see that she is very pregnant — perhaps eight months gone. What she must have been through, I know. And my heart has gone out to her unreservedly. I know I have something to say to her here tonight, words of comfort, of encouragement, of understanding, but right now I don't see how. I can't break into the group and drag her off. She and her little entourage are really tight in there. Looks impossible.

"Well, Father, you shall just have to work this one out. I

don't know how." I stand there by the phone lifting the whole scene.

Suddenly the pay phone rings at my shoulder. A gangling teenage boy walks over and answers it. He listens a few seconds and makes long steps to the table I am watching. He talks to her. My objective gets up and walks over right beside me to the telephone. It was for her. Praise the Lord! She comes to me. Thanks, Father. I sure couldn't have done it on my own.

She finishes talking, hangs up, and I address her.

"When are you having a baby?" I ask her.

"In about a month," she tells me.

"Are you in school?"

"Yes, in the ninth grade," she informs me. And we are off. I know I am here for her for I am filled with compassion. My heart has gone out to her. She is in a tough spot in her mind, but she is stubbornly hanging on to her togetherness. Should she keep the child or give it up for adoption? She shares her burdens.

God has made me able to meet her needs. For with God nothing shall be impossible. He can work that out too, I am telling her, so that you can make the best possible decision and be able to live with yourself whatever you decide. We talk more. Her face relaxes, her eyes are soft. She is comforted for He is the God of all comfort who comforts us in all our tribulation, that we may be able to comfort them which are in any trouble by the comfort wherewith we ourselves are comforted of God. Bless God.

Out of the corner of my eye, I see Dave beckoning to me. It's time to leave. I take her name, her address. She wants to know more. We say our good-byes. Her eyes are bathed by tears.

The six of us file out into the darkness of night, onto the street in Sidney. It doesn't matter where; it could be any-where — this is the world. This is the darkness where their eyes are blinded, and people are destroyed for a lack of knowledge — the knowledge of God.

No one says much in the car. It's a short drive to the next local hangout, just out of town. The blinking red and green Seven-Up sign marks the spot. Two of our cars are parked out front already.

Inside, it's one large, long room. Pool table at one end, small bowling alley in the back, a few pinball machines on one side, jangling of money, brassy tingling of the little ball. A juke box throws out a rainbow of colored lights and strains of rhythmic rock. On one end of the long room there is a bar presided over by a middle-aged lady in a bright green pant-suit.

We flock in. The place is full of saints. I'm overjoyed to see so many familiar faces again. It's as though we had taken over. The victory is ours before we even open our mouths. We mill around. We are there with a purpose, something beyond playing pool or staring at the girls or drinking beer or playing cards.

A young couple is ready to leave. Brian approaches them. "Going to another place?" he asks them. "No, that's it. We're going to bed," the guy says with a note of boredom. "Well, I have good news for you." Brian pronounces each word with relish, with enthusiasm. A few more words. They really don't care one way or the other. Apathy, good-byes. They leave.

Tim is talking to the tall mustached man, waiting to play pool. Tina is at the bar deep in conversation with two older men, their faces blank. Anyone who is not talking you just know is lifting the others, but most of our people are talking.

It's a weekday night. Not too many customers. Craig gets his car together to check out another place in town. The second car is set to go to the roller skating rink. We will meet here at 11:30.

The six from our car stay on. Eyeing the pool table, I sit down by two young men, both with large mustaches drinking beer at a little table. I crack open the conversation, "Been here before? What's happening in town?" Now Brian joins us, asking them a few questions about themselves.

The proprietress starts scolding Tina from behind the bar. "People come in here with all kinds of beliefs. Now it's none of my business. And stop bothering the customers. The Bible is for church on Sunday morning. Not for a bar."

Tina listens calmly. "Where the Bible really belongs is in

the mind. That's where it will do some good," Tina remarks simply.

The proprietress scolds someone else, "Don't talk about the Bible in here," I overhear her saying. And I recall how Jesus went and ate with the publicans and sinners, and how the Pharisees criticized Him for the company He kept, and how He said, "They that be whole need not a physician, but they that are sick." "I am not come to call the righteous, but sinners to repentance." That's where Jesus went – to the people who needed Him. If that was good enough for Him, it's good enough for us. "Sorry, Lady-in-green," I am thinking, but we're in the right place according to the Word. It doesn't matter what you think. You see, we ought to obey God rather than man. And the fact is, that none of the customers is bugged. They seem rather to be enjoying the conversation, the attention." But the lady can't stand it.

We are all decent and in order. She really has no complaints against us. Everyone is buying things to eat and drink. Everyone is talking quietly, behaving seemly. A man down the bar is arguing with the guy on his left. They have been drinking for a while, I gather, eyeballs kind of swimming, faces flushed red. The lady in green doesn't bat an eyelash. After a few moments the two men leave.

And the irony is that all that commotion can go on at the bar – maybe they're going out to kill each other – but there's nothing wrong with that so far as the lady dressed in green sees it. But to bring peace and love, to bring light into a dark place, the lady just can't handle it. Yes, we're in the right place.

Brian is still talking to the young man with the black mustache. He's fighting to get through apathy and inertia. The young man's eyes wander. He looks this way, that way. Finally he pulls some strands together to ask a question.

His friend sitting near me doesn't want to go on with the conversation. Hand-to-hand combat. He pushes his chair back in disgust.

"I got my church," he says visibly annoyed. "That's the Roman Catholic Church. They teach me there too. How do I know you're not the anti-Christ? Maybe you are. I don't have to talk to you guys."

"You're right," Brian responds. "That's a good question. How *do* you know we aren't the anti-Christ?" Brian throws it out and waits. The young man doesn't know.

"How about if you compare what I am saying to you with what the Bible says. If I'm just telling you what the Bible says and you believe the Bible, then we could just all rejoice in what we have in Christ. There's nothing to argue about." Never argue. Remember that from the tape. The young man curses, pushes a few choice phrases out from behind his teeth and stalks off to another table.

From the other end of the room, the unshaven pool player sits down across from me at my table.

"May I join you?"

"Sure, sit down." I don't say much, smile a lot. He begins to ask questions. He's heard of The Way. He wants to know how many people live there, where they come from, how they earn money, what they do — all sit around and BS about the Bible? I answer his questions.

"You could come up and see for yourself. That'll probably give you the best idea. Anytime," I invite him. "It's not far from here."

"What do you do there? How'd it get started? What kind of stuff do you teach?" he strings his questions out.

"We believe that the Bible is the Word of God."

"Yeh," he agrees. "I believe that too."

"And that the Word of God is the Will of God. After all, why should God say one thing to us and want us to do something else? He doesn't. He says what He means and means what He says."

"Sure, that makes sense," the unshaven man nods his head, wrinkling his eyebrows.

"So that's what we do up there — study and learn God's Word so that we can know His will for us, because when we know it, then we can do it. And God's will for us is always the best."

"Yeh, but I think there are a lot of ways to get to God," he tells me objectively.

"Jesus said, 'I am the way, the truth, and the life: no man

cometh unto the Father, but by me.' Now either He told the truth or He lied. If He lied, then He's a liar and we can't believe anything He said. But if He told the truth, then He is the *only* way. You can decide that for yourself."

The man slaps his knee and bursts into peels of laughter.

"You know, I never looked at it that way. Wow! Either He told the truth or He lied." The man stops to think and then bursts out laughing again, shaking his head back and forth. I know he has been blessed. A door has opened in his head.

"That's why we are called The Way, because we are all followers of Jesus Christ. He is the Way," I add in explanation.

More people come in. It's getting later. Those that have been here for a while are getting drunker. Here they are seeking warmth, comfort, companionship and light around the pool table, the TV set, around a deck of cards or at the bar, flipping the pinball machines or playing mini-bowling. What else is there to do on a midweek night in Sidney? Or anywhere? Get out of the house and have a few beers.

The proprietress in green hurries over to our table. Everyone is engaged, coming or going. The din of the sounds envelops the people.

"Stop bothering our customers now. Stop talking about the Bible," the lady in green admonishes me, her voice edged with anger.

I turn to the unshaven man across from me, who is still laughing to himself, shaking his head in amazement.

"Am I bothering you?" I ask him point-blank.

"No, no," he assures the green lady. The proprietress leaves us.

"Rosie sure looks after us. I'm a regular customer here, you see. She wants me to be happy, clucks around me like a mother hen."

That's nice she cares so much," I agree.

It is time to go. The joint has swung into motion. I see the young couple that left as we came in walking back through the door. Dave is already talking to them. Behind them, the other two carloads of our people have returned from town, from the skating rink. Their eyes are shining. They are smiling. We all enjoy seeing each other again. It's been a great night. Praise God. It's time to go.

We all gather orderly at the door and filter out by twos or threes into the night. We return in the same cars we came in. It was a heavy evening, I am thinking. I grope for understanding. It's detached from time and space, a spiritual place. We have been on a great spiritual military maneuver, a wedge of light driving into a world of darkness.

Today's battle is done. The troops have returned from the battlefield. They are mustered into formation. The roll has been called — none dead, none missing, none wounded. All soldiers present and accounted for. Having used up their alloted time and ammunition, the forces are regrouping to rest, to renew their strength in fellowship before the next onslaught. It was a spiritual invasion of the forces of light into the territory of the prince of darkness, and we have the victory. As light shines in any place, the darkness is shattered. It cannot stand or fight against light.

Today's battle is over. We are God's soldiers, God's army in a great spiritual encounter. God is our strength. Praise the Lord. It was a great night, a great fight. And we are ready for the next battle.

Dave drives in quiet confidence. In back the soldiers are sleeping. Beside me Sky looks out into the night. The sky is clear — the stars glitter, golden pinpoints in a vast canopy.

"Do you know that God called every star by name?" Sky says reflectively. "It's in one of the Psalms. Can you imagine that? We can't even see them all, even with a telescope, and it says that He tells the number of the stars, that He calls everyone by name. That's heavy. Sure is a big God."

We fall into silence the rest of the way. Dave drives. I am ecstatic in the stillness of the night. What a day. Another day in the Lord. Do you know that this has been the best day of my life? Do you know that tomorrow will be even better? Each day gets better in the Lord because God and His Word are the center of our lives, of this book and also of this place.

We are home. The car doors burst open, followed by a sprinkling of sleepy goodnights from the back seat. Dave lets us out by the Biblical Research Center and drives quietly to park the car behind the barn. I stand a moment under the one lit vapor lamp. The hollow echo of footsteps fades in the direction of Trailer 6 and Trailer 7.

I am alone — an athlete running the race, a soldier in a vast spiritual battle where light dispels all darkness, a tree planted by the rivers of water, that brings forth fruit in his season; and my leaf also shall not wither, and whatsoever I do shall prosper. The tree has grown from a seed that fell on good ground. And the seed is the Word of God. I am alone with God.

Is it 1 or 2 o'clock? I don't know. The night is warm and still. A full moon glows yellow above the trees. The breeze caresses my face, gentle as the finest silk. The damp and pungent smell of spring fills the air. A long winter is receding. Even in the dark, the nobby branches of the apple trees proclaim the blossoms of tomorrow, the fruits of the following day.

The good ground has thawed. It lies fresh, moist, fertile. A sower went out to sow his seed: and as he sowed, some fell by the wayside, and some fell upon a rock, and some fell among thorns, and other fell on good ground and sprang up. This is a place where the seed fell upon good ground. "For as the rain cometh down, and the snow from heaven, and returneth not thither, but watereth the earth, and maketh it bring forth and bud, that it may give seed to the sower, and bread to the eater: So shall my word be that goeth forth out of my mouth: it shall not return unto me void, but it shall accomplish that which I please, and it shall prosper *in the thing* whereto I sent it," saith the Lord. Light blazes in my mind.

The time is here. The time is now, when the fields shall spring forth with tender green wheat, when sweet william shall purple the forest floor, when the cows shall calve, when the apples shall ripen on the branch, and the Word shall bear fruit.

And I know that this place and this time is like that spoken of by the Prophet Isaiah:

The wilderness and the solitary place shall be glad for them; and the desert shall rejoice, and blossom as the rose.

It shall blossom abundantly, and rejoice even with joy and singing: the glory of Lebanon shall be given unto it, the excellency of Carmel and Sharon, they shall see the glory of the Lord, *and* the excellency of our God.

Strengthen ye the weak hands, and confirm the feeble knees.

Say to them *that are* of a fearful heart, Be strong, fear not: behold, your God will come *with* vengeance, *even* God *with* a recompence; he will come and save you.

Then the eyes of the blind shall be opened, and the ears of the deaf shall be unstopped.

Then shall the lame *man* leap as an hart, and the tongue of the dumb sing: for in the wilderness shall waters break out, and streams in the desert.

And the parched ground shall become a pool, and the

thirsty land springs of water: in the habitation of dragons, where each lay, *shall be* grass with reeds and rushes.

And an highway shall be there, and **a way**, and it shall be called **The way** of holiness; the unclean shall not pass over it; but it *shall be* for those: the wayfaring men, though fools, shall not err *therein*.

No lion shall be there, nor *any* ravenous beast shall go up thereon, it shall not be found there; but the redeemed shall walk *there*:

And the ransomed of the Lord shall return, and come to Zion with songs and everlasting joy upon their heads: they shall obtain joy and gladness, and sorrow and sighing shall flee away."

Isaiah 35

# *Epilogue*

Two and a half years have passed since the material for this book was gathered. Today once again I have the wonderful privilege of living at The Way International Headquarters in New Knoxville, Ohio, this time as a member of the Way Corps.

As the seed looks so different from the seedling, or the seedling from the mighty, growing tree, even so, many aspects of The Way ministry today are nearly unrecognizable. Everything has grown and expanded here — buildings, programs, operations, classes, departments, equipment and most of all — people.

People spoken of in this book who spent time here from all over the country have moved ahead, taken on greater responsibilities in areas all over the country and Europe. Some have married. Some have added children to their households. The spiritual family has grown. Others who were in the field are now living here, taking time to deepen their spiritual perception and their life's commitments to God and His Word. Truly, The Way tree is flourishing today as never before.

But, in spite of changes in outward appearances — in faces and numbers — the heart and the heartbeat, the pulse and the life, built on the accuracy and integrity of the Word of God, have remained the same. The heartbeat is more audible now, more distinct, since it is carried ever further by the growing body of believers acting on the truth. Facts have changed, but the truth of God's Word living in the heart of God's people and God's ministry are the same today as when the material was compiled.

I thank God for you, dear reader, for the time you have taken to visit here through these pages, and I take this opportunity to reiterate the invitation in the Introduction — come and see for yourself.

*Elena S. Whiteside*
*New Knoxville, Ohio*